THE
DON
JUAN
DILEMMA

THE DON JUAN DILEMMA

Should Women Stay with Men Who Stray

Jane F. Carpineto

WILLIAM MORROW AND COMPANY, INC.
New York

Grateful acknowledgment is made for the following excerpts:

"Gee, Officer Krupke" from *West Side Story*. Copyright © 1956, 1958, renewed 1984 and 1986 by Leonard Bernstein, Arthur Laurents, and Stephen Sondheim. Used by permission of Flora Roberts, Inc.

"Moonglow." Copyright © 1934 by Mills Music, Inc., c/o Filmtrax Copyright Holdings, Inc. Copyright renewed 1962 by Mills Music, Inc., and Scarsdale Music. International copyright secured. All rights reserved.

The Fitzgeralds and the Kennedys by Doris Kearns Goodwin. Copyright © 1986 by Doris Kearns Goodwin. Reprinted by permission of Simon & Schuster, Inc.

Rediscovering Love by Willard Gaylin. Copyright © 1986 by Willard Gaylin. All rights reserved. Reprinted by permission of Viking Penguin, a division of Penguin Books USA, Inc.

William F. May, Ph.D. "Four Mischievous Theories of Sex: Demonic, Divine, Casual, and Nuisance," in *Passionate Attachments: Thinking About Love* by Willard Gaylin, M.D., and Ethel Parson, M.D., eds. Copyright © 1988 by Friends of Columbia Psychoanalytic Center, Inc. Reprinted by permission of The Free Press, a division of Macmillan, Inc.

Library of Congress Cataloging-in-Publication Data

Carpineto, Jane F.
  The Don Juan dilemma: should women stay with men who stray
Jane F. Carpineto.
    p.   cm.
  Includes index.
  ISBN 0-688-08037-5
  1. Men—Sexual behavior. 2. Compulsive behavior. 3. Sexual
attraction. 4. Women—Psychology. I. Title.
HQ28.C37   1989
306.7'088041—dc19   89-3045
                                                                 CIP

Printed in the United States of America

    3 4 5 6 7 8 9 10

BOOK DESIGN BY KATHRYN PARISE

To my daughters,
Amy and Julie

ACKNOWLEDGMENTS

Although writing a book is primarily a solitary endeavor, there are always people who help make it happen and without whose assistance it wouldn't have happened. Without the help of my former editor and good friend Susan Victor and of Connie Clausen, the agent I dreamed of finding, this book would have been a fantasy instead of a reality.

I owe a debt of gratitude to my neighbor and friend Judy Quain, who read the manuscript several times from beginning to end—often on very short notice—and offered invaluable suggestions at every step of the way. Dr. George W. Goethals, professor of psychology at Harvard University, the instructor of the "Intimacy, Love and Loss" class, also read parts of the book and was generous in sharing his ideas with me in and out of class. My classmates, too, offered valuable insights as did Connie Clausen's associate, Susan Lipson.

There is no way that I can adequately thank the men and women whose privacy I invaded in order to learn about womanizing. Without their cooperation and generous contributions, there would have been no book at all. And had it not been for the patient tutelage of Elizabeth Brown of Softeach, I would not have mastered the intricacies of word processing. On more than one occasion, she saved me from near disaster.

Friends, family, and clients contributed immeasurably to this book with a combination of ideas and goodwill. My friends Linda Green and June Wolff took time out from their own busy schedules to assist me in integrating information. They, along with my husband, Joe, our two daughters, Amy and Julie, our friends Emily and Tom Lamont, Rita and Harry Pothoulakis, and numerous others of our friends, constituted the faithful cheering squad that every writer needs to complete a book.

Finally, I want to thank my editor, Lisa Drew, who with a few strokes of her pencil brought more clarity to the manuscript.

CONTENTS

INTRODUCTION

Womanizing is a modern word for an age-old practice. The refreshing thing about its usage is the implication inherent in the word—that we have made progress in our understanding of relations between the sexes. Today's "womanizers" were yesterday's "roués," "gallants," "ladies' men," Don Juans, and Casanovas. With the old labels these men could be perceived as romantic figures, as men who were helpless to prevent the adoration that they received from women and the secret envy that they inspired in less-appealing men. What woman wouldn't have fallen for Errol Flynn, and what man wouldn't have traded places with him?

When the tables take a turn, however, we find ourselves watching Dan, a character played by Michael Douglas, fall from grace for having indulged himself in an extramarital dalliance—a fatal attraction. Every bit as magnetic as the Don Juans of lore, Dan is robbed of the heroic stature they enjoyed. Now, Hollywood is telling us that Dan got himself into a mess, and there's no way for him to get out of it. He is responsible for the events and their tragic outcome. It's this new dimension of responsibility that converts him from a Don Juan to a womanizer. After seeing him in action, wouldn't a woman think twice before falling for him, and would any man want to trade places with him?

Finally, we're coming full circle to the darker side of Don Juanism. The use of the word "womanizer" has helped us along. It seems to be saying that men are doing something to women for which men are at least partially responsible, and it contains, with the suffix "ize," the suggestion of a habitual activity.

Of course, there have been words all along that speak directly to the dark side—words like "lecher" and "rake." The problem with these terms is that they lean too far to the dark side by placing all the blame on the errant man. The implication is that men who have bad characters are doing something to innocent women without their consent. Suppose we had become accustomed to referring to John Kennedy as a "lecher" or to Gary Hart as a "rake." That would have required us to regard them as men who were prone to forcing themselves upon unwilling women in order to obtain sexual favors. On the basis of available biographical evidence, we can only say in fairness that both men were "womanizers." They sought the company of women for social and sexual purposes, and were successful in pursuit to the extent that there were women who made themselves available.

Thus, the practice of womanizing connotes an activity in which men are the primary players because they initiate the action, control most of the plays, and choose a variety of women to be their partners in a succession of relationship games. Women are secondary players because they consent to participate. The womanizer as the primary player enters the activity with decided advantages. He is the aggressor and he is the man. As the aggressor, he assumes leadership in the interaction, and as the man, the upper hand has been accorded to him by tradition. The woman who chooses to involve herself with a womanizer is not powerless, however. She can accept or reject his advances. In doing so, she is making a decision, and regardless of the outcome of the relationship, she bears the kind of responsibility that accompanies all adult decisions. She is not a victim, but if she refuses to take responsibility for her actions, she will delude herself into thinking that she is.

This posture has psychological and political consequences for her. First, it can cause her to develop an exaggerated fear and resentment of men. Second, it does cause her to grant more power to men than they really have so that she plants herself as another roadblock on the march to equality for women.

Having said that womanizing is an activity that requires the willful participation of both men and women as well as mutual acceptance of responsibility, I want to place the spotlight back where it belongs—on men. Womanizers are men who have an irresistible urge to consort with women. Because the urge is irresistible, it can be called a compulsion. A compulsive behavior is one that cannot be inhibited even if the person tries or desires to control it. So a womanizer is a man with an irresistible urge and no self-discipline. Rather than control the urge, he allows the urge to control him. It leads him to desire women, and then to pursue the objects of his desire.

A true womanizer is a heartbreaker because he is never satisfied with one woman for very long. He is in perpetual search of greener pastures. At each stop he performs

a ritual ceremony of desire, pursuit, conquest, and dis-
appearance. Depending on the strength of the urge, he
may even perform the ceremony on several stages simultaneously. The more he plays the part, the more
skillful and successful he becomes. Women fall for him
with increasing frequency, and their admiration re-
charges his energy and strengthens the urge. Hence, there
are men who womanize well into senior citizenship.

If one were to ask an experienced womanizer why he
has devoted so much of his life to the pastime, he would
reply, "Because I love women." He says it because he
believes it in his conscious mind. The truth, however,
lies somewhere in the unconscious realm. Most men who
womanize don't dig deep enough to find it, but women
who have been hurt by womanizers are hungry for the
answer.

Women cannot conceive of womanizing as a man's
expression of his love for women. There has to be a darker
reason for such behavior—some kind of psychological
explanation—because women define true love as a bond
between one man and one woman. In the female psyche, love connotes a singular attachment. If her man has
dalliances, a woman will either use them as proof of his
having fallen out of love or will somehow find a way to
satisfy herself that she enjoys preeminence in his affections—the cat may stray, but he comes home to stay. She
may even go so far as to deny his transgressions, and
place all of her attention and blame on her rival. If, by
chance, the straying cat happens to be a woman instead
of a man, she will explain her behavior by saying that
she has fallen out of love with the man she is betraying,
or that the new lover has helped her to rediscover her
own dormant vitality. Rarely, if ever, have I heard a
woman say that she has affairs because she loves men.

There are, of course, women who "manize"—women
who go through a succession of amorous liaisons with

men without intentions of a commitment to any of them or awareness of the motives for their behavior. Still, there are not as many "manizers" in our midst as there are womanizers, and among the former, a good percentage will seek psychotherapy to help them overcome the practice. Eventually, a bell is likely to go off in their heads—a warning ring—signaling that something in the psyche isn't working properly.

Generally, women are more introspective than men and more relationship-centered. Thus, they turn to psychology as a way of making sense out of the complexities of male-female relationships. The widespread publicity that the subject of womanizing has received of late is a reflection of the elevation of female consciousness about an aspect of male behavior that has heretofore been swept under the rug or mired in romantic illusion. Thanks to a hardy band of mostly female journalists, a whistle has been blown, alerting the public that womanizers are men who just might have some character flaws.

Even though the whirlwind has mostly centered around whether womanizers are worthy of election to high public office, it has had a side effect as well. If we can't trust men like Gary Hart to govern us with honesty and integrity, can we trust them as husbands and lovers? It's a fair question, and it leads us to other disquieting questions: "Why do men womanize?," "Are there recognizable character traits in womanizers that are absent in other men?," "Why are womanizers so appealing to women?," "What kinds of women are good candidates for their attention?"

Insofar as women want the answers to these questions, this book is devoted to answering them, but it's not only answers to the "Whys" that women are seeking. The most important question of all is "What do I do about it?" If a woman loves a womanizer (as millions of women do), she's faced with a dilemma. Should she abandon him, wait for him to abandon her, or try to tame him? Are these her only choices? The hardest lesson for a psychotherapist to learn is that gaining insight is only half the client's battle. Eventually, some action must be taken.

Our discussion starts with insight and ends with action strategies. My aim is first to impart knowledge and secondly to help you apply the knowledge actively on your own behalf. Throughout these pages I assume that I, the writer, and you, the reader, have a mutual aim—the prevention of heartbreak.

PART 1

Background Music

CHAPTER 1

It Must Have Been Moonglow

American women are inundated with psychological information. It comes at them from every corner: from the magazine rack and the bookstore, from the local radio and TV talk show—from the likes of Sally Jessy Raphael, Donahue, and Oprah—from relatives and friends, and from the professional practitioners themselves—those benevolent people who dispense it for a fee. Nowadays, it is rare to meet an American woman who doesn't speak and think in the language of psychology with some degree of fluency.

To the extent that knowledge enhances growth, the psychological information explosion is a positive development. There is no question but that the 1980s woman is more self-aware and self-developed than her mother was. The new woman is apt to have opinions about who she is on the inside and what she wants from the world outside herself. She thinks that she has choices, and that the better she knows herself, the better equipped she will be to do the choosing. Thus, armed with self-aware-ness and assisted by the women's movement, she need not be as fatalistic as her mother. In a nutshell, that is the good news from the psychological front, but there is some bad news too.

The volume of such information directed at women far exceeds that directed at men. Marketing experts know that she reads more books and magazines, watches more daytime television, and listens to more radio talk shows than men do, but she doesn't know that these invisible wizards understand more about her habits than she does. She is convinced that she, along with millions of other American women, must be suffering from an amazing ar-ray of psychological distresses. Otherwise there would be no need for all this advice on how to get ahead in business, remain sexually attractive to her husband or lovers, and be a good parent to her children. Finally, she concludes that it is up to her to make life better for her-self and her loved ones. It is no wonder, then, that psy-chotherapists have grown accustomed to meeting scores of women who enter their offices saying, "There must be something wrong with me; my boyfriend doesn't want to marry me," "My husband never pays any attention to me," and/or "My kids are doing poorly in school." The assumption is that it's all her fault, and that the success of any relationship, be it romantic, professional, or pa-rental, is her responsibility. The media are not entirely to blame for this state of affairs, but they do capitalize on the female proclivity to focus more energy on rela-tionship issues than do men.

Furthermore, the assumption is more insidious than it looks. First, because it leads women to expect more from themselves than they can realistically deliver; second, because their willingness to take responsibility for relationship problems into their own hands means that someone else in the relationship is given permission to abdicate his share of the problem; and third, because many women never seek the professional help that could set them straight and so invite a certain amount of needless suffering.

The most important lesson women can learn from this book is that *it takes two to tango, not just you.* Sounds simple enough, doesn't it? It is as simple as it sounds, but it is also the most quickly forgotten lesson among all those that women have to learn. Think about it as you meet the following women who've all been involved with womanizers. Unlike most of the men whom you'll meet in later chapters, these women are psychological sophisticates. They've examined their own psyches and those of their lovers, and now they tell us why, despite all their insight, they've succumbed to the womanizer's allure.

Charm

Charm is that special something that some men have and other men lack. How many times have you heard yourself or your female friends describe a man as follows? "He has a way with women. When I'm with him, nothing else matters because he makes me feel that I am all that matters. He is so much fun. When I am with him, there's never a dull moment. He swept me off my feet. He has a sixth sense about my moods and feelings, my likes and dislikes." Every one of these phrases captures an essential ingredient in the charming man's gestalt. He knows how women feel and think, how to make them feel special, how to entertain them, how to arouse them, and how to identify and cater to their idiosyncrasies and vulnerabilities. He is the quintessential romantic—the man we spend our girlhoods dreaming about. He is the walking, talking, living, breathing personification of what we know as "Sex Appeal." He has a seventh sense—his innate ability to comprehend that the world is full of love-starved women who are extraordinarily receptive to a man's sexual signals. He is like the brownie that suddenly appears on the plate of the dieting woman. He is sugar and spice, IF *Only* he were nice! In brief, charm is the stuff that womanizers are made of.

As one woman told me:

"How could any woman resist Warren Beatty? If he beams his light, anybody will fall. These people [womanizers] have magnetism. They can make you feel so special. They can even make you feel a sense of power, as if you're a kind of sexual goddess. They're dazzling."

Now listen to another woman:

"I have been involved with two womanizers, and I come from a family of womanizers. For women, the attraction is fatal. A womanizer has so much charm that he makes you think you're special *because you have him*. When he shines his light on you, you get a surge of self-worth, and since you don't have self-esteem to begin with, you're dependent on him to recharge the battery. His biggest victim, then, is the woman who can't be alone because she doesn't like herself well enough to be in her own company."

Both of these women are successful professionals who came to the brink of letting go of the good, but much less *charming*, men they are involved with now. The first

woman reached the age of thirty-five before her insights
about womanizers caught up with her own behavior. As
she put it, "I finally had an epiphany. I stopped falling
for these men." It took the second woman a little longer,
past the forty mark, before she allowed herself to be in
a stable relationship with a man.

Other women are not so fortunate:

Sally: "Womanizers are shallow and insecure, but they're
charming and fun so you get swept away."

Carol: "Womanizers are not just charming. They're
daring and exciting too."

Martha: "Womanizers are charming and fun to be with.
I fall for the fun as much as for the charm."

Joan: "They all have this relaxed way with women.
They're charming and easy to be with. They're funny.
They're kids, and when you're with them it's OK to be
a kid. It's fun to be irresponsible and silly. They're
passionate and physical. It's an effort to be attracted to
a real nice, solid guy. I have to be on my best behavior
with one of them."

None of these four women has found a satisfactory way
out of her entanglement with womanizers. Sally and
Martha have been too badly burned by their philandering men to dare take steps to find more gratifying relationships with new men. Carol and Joan are ambivalent
about changing their behavior. They're unconvinced that
other women enjoy happier relationships with less dazzling men. Before you decide that Carol and Joan are
right, let's take a look at charm from another angle.

In addition to his prominence as the father of modern
psychiatry, Freud was famous for his one-liners. He once
said to an amused audience, "A cigar is only a cigar," by

which he meant that there need be no additional meaning or interpretation attached to a cigar beyond what it obviously is—a cigar. The same could be said about charm. Sometimes it is only charm. According to the dictionary, that means "a trait that fascinates or allures." As you have just seen, however, some women attach more meaning to it than it deserves. For such women, a man with charm is not a man with a trait, but rather a man who is larger than life. He appears as a savior might, as someone endowed with wondrous magical powers, who, with a wave of his wand, can give a woman self-esteem, joy, sexual vitality, and all the love, affection, and attention that she will ever need.

A charming man, in reality, is a dangerous man for any woman, because she can't isolate what he *has* (that is, a specific character trait) from who he *is*. Charm, when seen for what it is, is a pleasant, social quality. It enables the person who possesses it to be relaxed and engaging in his interactions with others, and it tends to elicit positive, reciprocal responses from them. It is a social skill, and that's all it is. Most of us can get along very well in life without it. It's a useful quality if you're a person who gets enjoyment from attending parties, or if you happen to have the kind of job that requires you to sell ideas or products to a wide variety of people.

The problem with charm is that the person who has it receives so much instantaneous, positive feedback that he overplays his hand. He relies more and more on his charm to get him past life's hurdles, and ignores or fails to develop other, more vital, human qualities—integrity, honesty, courage, sincerity, intimacy.

One of the best descriptions of the up and down sides of charm as a character trait is contained in Doris Goodwin's book, *The Fitzgeralds and the Kennedys*. Writing about the young Jack Kennedy when he was a hospital-bound three-year-old stricken with scarlet fever and separated from his family, she says:

Throughout the long ordeal of his separation from his family, young Jack Kennedy displayed a remarkable character trait which served to lessen his emotional loss and which stayed with him the rest of his life. The portrait of the little boy that emerges from the letters of the hospital nurses is that of an irresistibly charming child with an uncommon capacity to stir emotions in people, creating in each of them the feeling that he and they somehow shared a special bond.[1]

Kennedy, as we all know, was a charming man who did not rely exclusively on his charm to make his way in life, but as we also know, he was a womanizer—a man who had considerable difficulty with intimacy. Goodwin goes on to say:

Younger and smaller than his favored brother Joe Junior, Jack perhaps had learned at an even earlier age how to reach out beyond his parents, to his aunts and uncles, his maids and his governesses—and now to the nurses for the affection he craved. For him, reaching out to others in the larger world promised salvation; yet *even as he charmed people one by one, drawing friends to his side as if by magic,* he would retain a measure of reserve, an avoidance of easy intimacy, which, in the strange alchemy of his relationships, served only to increase his attraction to others.[2]

Herein lies the answer to the riddle of the charming man. More often than not he uses his charm to receive rather than to give, and as he continues to attract people to him, he retreats from those he has attracted. The unsuspecting woman, then, fails to understand that *his* charm doesn't offer *her* anything. It is a way of getting attention which masquerades as a way of giving it.

Charm is only a trait, but unfortunately, as was the case with Kennedy, it appears to be more prevalent in love-hungry men than in love-generous men. From my personal and professional experience, I have observed that men who love women don't cultivate their personal charm. If they have it, it's almost imperceptible—a background light. In the true charmer, it's apparent—a floodlight. A womanizer displays his charm in neon.

Fun

Along with his charm, the typical womanizer has a playful spirit. "He's so much fun to be with," exclaims every woman who has kept company with a womanizer. "After you've spent time with a womanizer, other types of men seem dull and boring," they hasten to add. However varied these women's definitions of fun may be, collectively they see in the womanizer an extraordinary talent for creating fun. For them, he has a special entertainment value. He's a "good time" guy, and is likely to remain so throughout the courtship stage, but thereafter he is apt to change his colors—sometimes abruptly.

Laura remembers:

"I was never allowed to date until I left home. I felt I had missed a lot of good times, so I rejected the nice, regular guys in favor of the good time guys. I married one of them at twenty-three. At first, it was a barrel of fun. He knew I'd never been anywhere, so he got a big kick out of entertaining me and taking me to new places, but as soon as I wanted more seriousness in our relationship, he withdrew from me. He had to be having fun all the time so he started seeing other women."

Laura's story was repeated to me many times by other women. During childhood, adolescence, and early adulthood, they had not had many opportunities for fun, so they were attempting to make up for lost time by attaching themselves to fun-loving men who could give them their first taste of a good time. They were easy prey for womanizers.

In their relationships with women, womanizers do not display a seriousness of purpose. Enjoyment is the sum and substance of a relationship for them, and when the enjoyment fades, the relationship withers along with it. Womanizers define enjoyment in sexual terms. They say: "As long as the sex is fun, the relationship will last but when it stops being fun, it's over."

While women also speak of "fun" in the sexual context, their definition is usually not confined to it. For women, "fun" means adventure, new experiences, romance, laughter, and enjoyable activity (all of which are inclusive and exclusive of sex). Womanizers are adept at satisfying this female appetite for fun as a *prelude* to obtaining their own sexual version of fun.

This linking of fun and romance begins in high school when the "party" boys win all the popularity awards and capture all the pretty girls, leaving the less favored boys standing by in awe and envy. Whether or not their perception is accurate, the onlookers assume that the popular boys are more sexually experienced and savvy than they are, and that sexual conquest is the reward they receive for their "fun" personalities. Once these high school heroes have advanced to manhood, most of them grow weary of the partying and settle into more serious pursuits. Some never do, and among those a good proportion who were once teenage "girlizers" become adult womanizers. Sooner or later too, most of the awestruck, envious boys date, court, and marry. A few, still stung by their adolescent romantic failures, become womanizers.

I think a very good case can be made for the idea that many American women carry over an idealized image of the popular party boy into adult life and allow it to serve as their male love model, either in an attempt to re-create the dynamic intensity of adolescent fun and passion or to find it for the first time. The game changes, however. Fun and romance in adolescence are unencumbered with the burden or the expectation of permanence, whereas in adult life they are perceived as criteria for commitment. With womanizers, fun and romance are as short-lived as they were in adolescence, but for many women, the "fun" guy remains in her imagination as the most lovable of the species.

Challenge

Every woman who has loved a womanizer speaks directly or indirectly about the challenge he presents to her. Usually, this challenge comes at the point in the relationship when Mr. Wonderful begins to reveal his true erratic colors, when he is less consistent in his attentiveness to her. Although this is the precise juncture where she should post warning flags for herself, strange as it may seem, she is apt to do the opposite. His retreat sends her a green light, and she pursues him with renewed energy. This phenomenon has been discussed by so many writers, most notably by Robin Norwood, Susan Forward, Connell Cowan and Melvyn Kinder, that it doesn't warrant much repetition except as it applies to women in pursuit of womanizers. In this context, the important thing to emphasize is that the womanizer, with his compulsion to philander, is an impossible man to catch. He can't be caught. Whether he marries her or not, sooner or later his elusive nature will get the better of him. What is phenomenal is that it may be a very long time indeed before his behavior wears her down.

The woman who loves a womanizer has endurance. She thrives on the challenge that he offers her. "If I can win him, I have scored a major victory. Then I will have proven that I'm the fairest of them all," she tells herself. Here are some tales of challenge brought to you directly from the front:

"When he'd back off, I'd pursue. I liked the cat-and-mouse game. I wanted to win out."

"I loved the challenge. I'd be able to prove once and for all that I was the powerful, wonderful, good one that he'd been waiting for."

"These guys are manipulating you. You're a walk-on, walk-off part on their stage, but you keep pushing for the lead part."

These quotes speak for themselves. They're the voices of women who have endured or are continuing to endure the challenge. One senses in these women a strong spirit of competitiveness as if they hope, through winning, to prove their worthiness; as if competition is the only avenue that they believe can take them to the safe haven of self-esteem.

Perhaps we can blame some of this equating of winning and worthiness on popular culture, which reinforces the idea that if you're better at something than the next person you must be a better person. However, I don't think that is the primary motivation for the addiction to challenge that we see in these women. I think it is correlated with the scores that were left unsettled with their fathers—a subject I will address extensively in the next chapter.

But whether or not the root cause for the allure of the

challenge can be traced back to their relationships with their fathers, the fact remains that for every woman who loves a womanizer, adventure comes with the territory. Although it is not necessarily the whole of it, the challenge is a big part of the adventure. Suspense supplements the challenge. Every womanizer can be counted upon to keep a woman guessing about where she stands with him. Drama is guaranteed. He will carry her through a range of emotions that she never knew she had, and at a level of intensity as thrilling as anything that Disneyland can offer—dips and twirls, whirlwind highs and lows, speed and sound, laughter and terror; all that and more until it's over. Who wouldn't try to catch a man who can do all that, you well may ask? My answer: "A woman who doesn't want to live life on a roller coaster."

Caregiving and Caretaking

People often wonder why young women barely out of adolescence become attracted to men old enough to be their fathers, or why women of any age become attracted to men with problems. Part of the reason for this may be credited to the changes that have taken place in our society since the end of World War II. In days gone by, we could rely on our families, communities, and churches to function as our support systems. As we have moved farther away from our geographical roots, however, we have come to rely exclusively on the "significant others" in our lives—the people closest at hand—to serve as replacements for the supports we have left behind. We turn to our spouses and lovers, and lay our unmet needs and our emotional expectations at their feet. These people become too significant, because we expect more from them than they can possibly offer us. Our romantic relationships become setups for disappointment. Some women go to extremes with their hopes and expectations because they have exaggerated dependency needs.

So the twenty-two-year-old woman who strolls on the arm of her forty-two-year-old lover is silently asking him to be both husband and father as is the fifty-year-old woman who stays married for thirty years to her irresponsible, little-boy husband. The first one expresses her need to be cared for directly while the second one does it indirectly. Here I am saying that the woman who asks to be cared for and the woman who gives care are one and the same. They are showing different faces of the same coin. The first one says, "Take care of me." The second one says, "I'll give you the care that I have always longed to receive. By feeling needed, I will feel attached and loved."

Womanizers are appealing candidates for the role of significant other to the overdependent woman. Alongside their "take-charge" quality, their adventurousness, and their charm, womanizers offer overdependent women a sense of kinship. Both are love-starved human beings. Their mutual starvation is the essence of the sexual chemistry between them, but neither of them has a conscious awareness that it is starvation that accounts for their magnetic attraction to one another.

A person who has not received love is not very good at giving love. Deprivation produces greed, not generosity, and since the love-hungry partners both want more than they can give, they are forced into pretending that they are givers instead of takers. The necessity to deceive one another makes them creative actors on the romantic stage. If we listen to a few women, we will learn more about the duet that women and their womanizers perform:

"I'm really a very dependent person who wants to be taken care of. Womanizers fill the bill for me, because I can look independent by not making too many demands on them, but I can get taken care of too because I ask for so little that they appreciate me and do things for me just because I haven't asked."

This woman disguises her dependency by not making demands, and her partners conceal their dependency by doing favors for her in the knowledge that there are no strings attached. She is too afraid to ask for what she wants for fear her man will leave her. She exhibits the "Half a loaf is better than no loaf" kind of dependency. Here is another kind of dependent woman who was married to a womanizer:

"I was inexperienced when I met him. We had a karmic relationship. He was romantic and European and very polite to me. He made me feel cared for and protected from the outside world. He played the protector and the macho man, and gave me all the money I needed. I was never allowed to ask about his whereabouts. He made it clear that he was the boss and the king, and that I shouldn't question his word. Now that we're separated, I'm coming out of the pain I've experienced with him, but I'm not sure that I wouldn't fall for it again."

The karmic quality of this relationship is an example of the chemistry I have referred to. Like dogs, these people sniffed each other out and mated. She wanted a protector, and he wanted to play the part of protector for *her* and the little boy in search of love with *other women*. In reality, they were birds of a feather. Her dependency is the straightforward "I want a Daddy" variety. As the parade goes forward, we meet another type:

"The womanizers I have loved have all had this quality of making me feel that they'll take care of me. They
will make up for everything I lack: connections, satis-
factions, adventure. If I go to the mountains alone, I'll
see despair and loneliness, but if I go with an exciting
man—a caretaker—I'll see all the positive things. They
give you the dessert and ignore the meat and pota-
toes."

For her, womanizers serve another caretaking purpose. She looks to them to supply her with everything
she lacks. Feeling as if she is one half a person, she finds
"despair" and "loneliness" in her own presence. She is
an example of someone who sees the womanizer as a
savior, and her need of him supplies fuel for his insatiable ego. Her dependency is reminiscent of the partially
completed jigsaw puzzle that sits on the table. It is the
"Please complete me" type. The parade goes on:

"I fell for the charm and the fun and the lost soul pitch.
Even though the relationships ended when all the cards
were faceup, I went around feeling that these men
would never forget me. In their hearts, there would
always be a place for me. They made me feel important, and I still need to feel that way. They were emotional cripples."

Last but not least comes the caregiver—the woman who
needs to be needed. In this scenario, she is the lead actor playing the part of the giver while yearning to be the
taker. She is attracted to the emotionally crippled kind
of womanizer, but behind her mask she herself feels
emotionally crippled and deprived. In her fantasies, she
is still at the center in these men's hearts—beloved by
them forevermore. The form that her dependency takes
can be called "I'll give anything to have your love."
Excessive dependency needs come in so many vari-

eties and disguises in men and women these days that it would be impossible to list all of them here. The above examples are among the most common. We know that women traditionally put more eggs in the basket of relationships than men do. Thus, their dependency problems are more obvious and better understood. Suffice it to reiterate, for our purposes, that overdependent women are easy targets for womanizers. They can't resist what such men *appear* to offer, because womanizers always present themselves in sugarcoated disguises. Rarely do they appear awkward, unsure of themselves, timid or shy. On the contrary, their appeal lies in their ability to *take charge* of the interaction with a woman. When a woman is too dependent, she wants someone to take over. She wants to surrender—to leave her fate in someone else's hands. That, in fact, is her definition of love.

All of us begin life with the same definition. As infants, we must surrender to our parents, but as we grow (given, of course, that we have received enough love and encouragement), we come to view love more as an experience of *sharing* than of *surrender*. The woman who has been unable to cross the bridge from surrender to sharing, as the result of the withholding of parental love, stands duty at a lookout post waiting for potential caretakers. Womanizers sell themselves as willing, eager, and ideally suited to the task.

When you compare what men say later in this book about their motivations for womanizing with what the women have just said about the reasons that they're attracted to womanizers, you will see some striking differences. The majority of women speak in psychological terms. They identify their own vulnerabilities and talk about the way those vulnerabilities become susceptible to the womanizer's psychological manipulations. There is a tacit understanding among all of them that womanizers are long on style and short on substance. Because they were better students of psychology, there were more women who were able to break out of their relationships with womanizers than womanizers who were able to stop womanizing.

Still, as I said in the Introduction, insight only assists recovery. It doesn't guarantee it. Among the women I interviewed for this book, along with many others I have worked with as a therapist, there are a certain number who are unable to convert insight into action. This, I believe, is because the compulsion to repeat the pain of the past over and over again, in the vain hope that the new replay will right the old wrongs, is very often so powerful a force in human beings that it overwhelms the ability of insight to change behavior. For an illustration of this phenomenon, known as *repetition compulsion,* I return again to Doris Goodwin writing about the effect of Joseph Kennedy's affair with Gloria Swanson on the lives of his sons:

> Yet there is little denying that the Swanson affair had a permanent effect on the Kennedy family, for history would later record a connecting link between the risks Joseph Kennedy took with Gloria Swanson and the sexual daring that would be observed again and again in his sons. It would seem almost as if, in repeating their father's behavior, they were unconsciously trying to gain some sort of mastery over this early trauma that had nearly destroyed everything they had.[3]

The stronger the compulsion is, the harder it will be to unravel it, and without intensive psychotherapy (several years of it) the prognosis is pessimistic.

For single women there is one factor, however, that often can compete successfully against the repetition compulsion—the biological clock, the wish to procreate. If a woman's desire to have a baby is strong enough, she will very likely trade in her womanizer for a less dazzling Daddy for her babies. Often, she will have needed psychotherapy to bring her to this critical choice.

The Unspoken Motivators: Power and Protection

Finally, we focus on a subject that was noticeably absent in my interviews with women, and barely touched upon by the men: power. Sometimes what is unsaid is as interesting as what is said, and to be a kind of unmentionable topic, something that nice people don't discuss. Of course, there were allusions to it when men spoke of their desire to "control" women or women confessed that they liked men who "took care" of them. Even the magnetism of the womanizer's charm and the challenge he poses have some connection to power since both charm and challenge are represented as qualities that *weaken* a woman's resistance. When they used the word "control," the men were referring to their desire to orchestrate the relationship rather than using it to connote the wish to dominate or exercise authority over a particular woman Not one man said, in terse, straightforward language, that he enjoyed power and domination, nor did any woman say that she was attracted to a womanizer for the power he projected. In contrast to the answers I received to "prickly" questions on other matters, the responses about power were decidedly oblique. In my view, there is an obvious explanation for this curious omission: The love of power is the womanizer's first and only true love, and his best-kept secret. Power and promiscuity go hand in hand whereas love and power are antithetical. The womanizer uses promiscuity as a way to ward off love.

Fearing that love will return him to a state of helplessness not unlike that he experienced as a child vis-à-vis his mother, he seeks to dominate women rather than take a risk with love. His ego isn't strong enough to take the chance of being overwhelmed and overpowered by a woman. As we will see in a later chapter, most womanizers have had troubled relationships with their mothers. With no reservoirs of trust to draw on, they regard women as objects of fear rather than of love. The womanizer, then, takes extraordinary care never to reveal his inner helplessness. He poses instead as someone who exudes power and control from every pore.

To some extent his charade obtains aid and comfort from the mixture of adoration and enmity that we Americans bestow upon the man of power. While we say out of one side of our mouths that a man is dishonorable if he pursues power as both a means and an end, from the other side we envy and admire him for having attained all the trappings of power—and we don't seem to mind how he did it.

The best-kept secret among women in America is that as much as they say they don't want to be dominated by powerful men, either at home or at work, when they are placed in the romantic arena, a significant number, maybe even a majority, are riding around on the coattails of just such men or anxiously awaiting the opportunity to do so. I don't believe, though, that it is domination they're seeking from these men. I think they're looking for protection from the cares and stresses of the cruel, hard world. Asking for protection is equivalent to saying, "I am the weak one. You are the strong one." What they fail to grasp is that when they look for *protection* from men, they're likely to get *domination* instead. The men who step into the role are liable, in most instances, to be the kind of men who love power. While I would not contend that all power-loving men are womanizers, I would not hesitate to assert that all womanizers are power lovers, and that the women who love them secretly wish to be protected. Women cannot have it both ways. They can't have love and protection at the same time, because love is a bond between equals. Once a hierarchy is established, the bond becomes one of power rather than love.

In the process of writing this chapter I had an opportunity to talk at some length with a sophisticated Frenchwoman about the differences between a French womanizer and his American counterpart. This is what she had to say about power:

"American men womanize because they love power. They want to strut. Look at all these American businessmen who reach middle age and then go out seeking young women. Before long they divorce their wives and go off with one of these sweet young things. They're living with a delusion. It's power they're after—not sex. Sex is easy to obtain. In France they do it because it's understood by men and women alike that sex with the same partner gets tiresome after ten years of marriage, so when a man goes out in search of women, he's looking for sex and that's all. There's even an expression for it, 'un cinq à sept'—'between five o'clock and seven o'clock.' He's very discreet about it. He doesn't disrupt the family with it. If a woman has an extramarital affair or two, she behaves the same way, but women don't seek new sexual experiences as often as men do. Of course, here I'm speaking about the upper class. Frenchmen in the lower social classes are inclined to go to prostitutes. In France, prostitutes are not regarded as they are in America, as the scum of the earth. They're more like romantic characters. Irma La Douce is a good example. Now if we're talking about men in high political positions, then it's the same the world over. These are men who womanize because they love power."

CHAPTER II

Our Hearts Belong To Daddy

Thoughts About Fathers and Daughters

For several years I have entertained a ridiculous fantasy, one that both amuses me and piques my curiosity. I picture myself mailing a questionnaire to every woman over sixty-five, on which there would be only one request: "Looking back over your life, choose one man among all the men you have ever known who you feel has had the most significant impact on your life and identify his relationship to you—father, husband, lover, son, grandfather, uncle, brother, or other." I imagine myself opening stacks of envelopes, with almost every one containing the answer: "My FATHER had the most significant impact on my life." So after days or weeks of opening and stacking, when the FATHER pile extended from floor to ceiling, I'd sit back smugly and tell myself, "See, I told you so," which would be followed by, "You wasted a lot of time and money trying to find out what you already knew."

You know that your fathers have been major players in your own life dramas, but do you know how much time you may have wasted learning the heartbreaking way that many of your misfortunes in love are attributable to your life with father and not to your life with any or all of your lovers? Of course, you have known this all along, but rather than heed your own counsel, you convinced yourselves that experience was a better teacher for you than you could be for yourself. So you proceeded to submit yourselves to painful romantic experiences, most of which were unnecessary, because you knew before the odyssey began (even if you didn't admit it) that without settling your score with father, you were inviting a lot of misery with men.

Dr. William Appleton is a psychiatrist and a columnist for *Cosmopolitan* magazine, and in the introduction to his book *Fathers and Daughters,* he explained that his motivation to write it came from the mail he received from unhappy women who were readers of his column. He noticed that their letters contained descriptions of their problems with lovers but that they failed to mention their fathers as contributors to their adult unhappiness. Thinking that this was a curious omission, he decided to interview eighty-one women in depth about the effects of their relationships with their fathers on their adult lives.

From them I discovered that they did realize the importance of paternal influence but saw no application for the knowledge. Consequently they had no reason to volunteer observations about their fathers. A pattern emerges. When queried, young women often reported an inability to sustain intimacy, enjoy success, and advance confidently in their careers. Questioned further they often described their fathers quite perceptively. Yet they failed to undo his negative influence from the past in order to overcome their present difficulties.[1]

It is true, as noted in Chapter I, that it is sometimes difficult for women to utilize psychological information to their advantage. They may be able to diagnose their own problems, but treating them is another matter altogether, one that is usually left in the hands of experts, whose services are apt to be expensive, time-consuming, and hard to sell to many women, especially those over thirty or thirty-five who are racing against the clock to put their love lives in order. This, by the way, is precisely why the self-help concept is so appealing to women, as evidenced by the popularity of self-help books and the spread of support groups for women.

There is also room for a feminist perspective in any discussion of fathers' roles in their daughters' love problems as a complement to a psychological orientation. Women need to become fully aware about the ways in which their historical second-class citizenship has impaired their ability to trust their own wisdom. In the post–women's liberation era, it is common to hear women say that they didn't really *come into their own* until mid-life. Undoubtedly, one reason for this is that discrimination tends to stunt the victim's natural rate of growth and increases her capacity to *tolerate* the inopportune conditions that are the consequence of discrimination.

It was interesting, therefore, to listen to men and women who described their mothers as "strong." They used the term in reference to the ability to put up with hardship as opposed to the ability to assert themselves in the interest of personal development and fulfillment.

By this definition, feminine strength meant sacrificing one's own needs and goals. Not so, however, when applied to fathers, for whom strength was defined in connection with self-assertion and personal success. These definitions, shared by men and women alike, are good illustrations of how effectively discrimination colors our collective perceptions. Clearly, we judge our mothers and fathers by unequal standards.

Your father provided your first and most important exposure to someone who was a first-class citizen. Maybe he was a wimp, maybe an autocrat, a father beloved or a father detested, a husband mother adored or a husband she endured, but in the final analysis he was the man who would become the hero or the villain for your own romantic saga. No matter if it was the best of times or the worst of times, you lived with him (or without him) at the most formative and impressionable stage of your life, at a time when he was the strong one, and you were the weak one, and very likely in an era when fathers were kings because mothers had no power to compete for the throne. In later years, once you have departed the kingdom, the way that your father used or abused his inherited power in relation to you will serve to define the parameters of your relationships with men.

This is a roundabout way of highlighting the reasons why many a woman's love life still centers around Daddy: Women who have an established pattern of loving womanizers are the daughters of fathers who abused their power in one way or another. The abuse of power can take many forms. Fathers can be, at one extreme, cruel, domineering, sexually or physically abusive, neglectful or emotionally distant toward their daughters or, at the other extreme, so doting, invasive, and enmeshed with their daughters as to give the appearance of a need to be idolized. Among the fathers of the women I interviewed, all of these extremes were represented.

Thoughts About Mothers and Daughters

On the one hand, our lovesick female clients tell us that their mothers, far more than their fathers, were the adults they felt they could count on for the meeting of basic survival needs as well as for many of their psychological needs. On the other hand, as adult daughters, they reveal a subtle disdain and lack of respect for their mothers for having sacrificed so much on the altar of marriage. Despite the fact that in many instances their fathers' behavior as husbands, parents, and family providers was far more reprehensible than their mothers', these daughters, in hindsight, show less forgiveness and compassion for their mothers than they do for their fathers. This clinical impression contains the sting of injustice. Mothers, so it would seem, take more than their share of blame for their daughters' romantic misfortunes.

Adult daughters often judge their mothers by today's standards rather than by those that prevailed at a time when women had fewer choices and opportunities than are now available. Furthermore, the problem is compounded by the fact that most of the great psychological thinkers and theorists were products of the old male-dominated order, and while their work represents a modernization and modification of Freudian thinking, Freud's essential framework is still in place. Mothers are still viewed as the primary parent, and the resolution of the oedipal complex is still regarded as a vital passage in human development.

For both girls and boys, the pre-oedipal period is characterized by the attachment to the mother, but at the start of the oedipal period mother and daughter become rivals for the father's affection. During this phase of her growth, the girl transfers her affection from mother to father. Eventually, the daughter must acknowledge that her father belongs to her mother and forsake her rivalry with the mother to return to a new alliance with her—an alliance that calls for her to forge a positive identification with the mother. Whereas the boy has only one switch to make in his oedipal journey, the switch from loving mother to identifying with the "good and generous" father, the girl has to make two switches, the first from mother to father, the second from father back to mother. In Chapter IV, we will learn about the perils that can befall the boy as he proceeds on his less complicated oedipal journey, but let's look now at what can happen to the girl:

1. She can have an insecure bonding with mother in the pre-oedipal period, leaving her with unresolved anger and frustration toward the mother, which she will carry into the oedipal position.

2. The rivalry with the mother may be aborted (through death, illness, desertion, or the mother's passivity, which permits a too-close bonding between daughter and father) exaggerated (through jealousy or vengefulness against the daughter for receiving too much attention from the father), or sabotaged by the father (by excessive negativity toward or cruel rejection or abuse of his daughter).

3. The identification process may be too negatively charged to be completed successfully either because of the buildup of pre-oedipal anger, the above rivalry complications, or the mother's personal liabilities as a positive role model for her daughter. For the purposes of this discussion, this third point is the most important since presumably it is the source of the continuing resentment and unforgiveness toward mothers that we see in our female clients.

One can argue with some of the bathwater features of the oedipal theory without throwing out the baby. The bathwater is the idea of the primacy of the mother in this age of increasing participation by the father. The baby, in my opinion, is the indisputable fact that daughters have to find some way to secure a positive feminine identification in order to sustain a gratifying love relationship with a man. Ideally, this happens when mother and daughter forge a positive connection, but in its absence the daughter must either find a substitute feminine role model with whom she can identify or arrive at a truce with her mother by grieving for what she didn't get from her and then redeeming the relationship through forgiveness and compassion.

As female psychotherapists, my colleagues and I are often called upon to serve as mother stand-ins for adult daughters. If we are lucky enough to be liked and admired by them, we can sometimes accomplish two tasks at once by replacing negative role models *and* facilitating the grieving and the forgiveness for the mother's original sins. If a happier, more loving and lovable daughter is the result, we rejoice, but we know before we begin that it won't happen overnight.

Families of Women Who Love Womanizers

One way of looking at both normal and dysfunctional families is through the lens that family therapists use. They view the family as a circular system containing feedback loops that relay verbal and nonverbal messages back and forth between family members. This means that every member of the family is an integral part of the system and that all members are affected by the behavior of each individual in the family.

A healthy family is a flexible systemic structure which allows for individuality and connectedness at the same time and sends "in-house" messages to that effect. Roles are not rigid. A vibrant marital relationship is the centerpiece of family activity. Sometimes Dad takes out the trash. At other times he makes the beds. He and Mom are comfortable switching roles. One son likes art, the other baseball, and the daughter wants to be an engineer when she grows up. These individual differences are acknowledged and supported by family members.

In an unhealthy family, roles are locked in so that freedom of motion and expression is obstructed. Family members have to short-circuit their individuality in order to maintain a homeostatic balance in the family. The marital relationship is rigidly defined. Dad performs only the "man's" jobs, and he requires his sons to be athletes. Mom does the "woman's" things, and both Mom and Dad reinforce their daughter's "feminine" characteristics and negate any "masculine" interests she may have. Under these circumstances, the family is like a computer that operates by means of preprogrammed codes. The families of women who love womanizers, like those of the womanizers themselves, are characterized by these rigid role definitions.

When talking about their childhoods, women are apt to speak in "systems" language. That is, they make more references than men do to the ways in which the behavior of one or another family member affects everyone in the family. Their eyes and ears are tuned to what I call "relationship fallout," the spreading of dysfunctional marital and/or parental relationship debris to a variety of family recipients.

Distant Fathers—Depressed or Martyred Mothers

If a daughter experiences her father as distant, the chances are better than average that her mother will have the same impression of him. There are many ways a man can distance himself from his family. One obvious way, rather typical of American men, is to bury oneself in work. This practice is so common in our country that we have given it semiclinical status by labeling it "workaholicism"—a term that wasn't part of the everyday vernacular during the childhood spans of the women I interviewed. Well over half of them referred to their hardworking fathers as "absentee fathers"—men who spent long hours at work and short ones at home. In the majority of cases, absenteeism and emotional distance were linked, with the implication that the absence produced the distance, that is, that the necessity to work hard as the family provider prevented the father from being close to his family. For blue-collar fathers, this explanation for distance carries more weight than it does for higher-paid white-collar fathers (who represented the majority of fathers).

To a psychologically oriented reader, the explanation will sound suspicious, not only with respect to the potential for confusing cause and effect (it's just as plausible that a father's inability to be intimate causes him to spend more time at work) but also because it appears as an unconscious device for giving fathers somewhat more credit than they deserve—an example of the way that daughters demonstrate the tendency to be more forgiving toward their fathers than their mothers. Regardless of how one might interpret the absentee-distance connection, the daughters were painfully aware of the effects it had on their mothers as well as on themselves and their siblings. A woman I'll call Julie described her family as follows:

"My father was the absentee kind. He worked long hours, but he was also a drinker and a womanizer. That was his idea of manliness. When he was home he never listened to us. He did all the talking. He was a charmer, a funny and appealing personality, but he didn't show this side of himself to the family, especially to his adolescent daughters. My mother's idea about marriage was that you had to endure it, you had to pay a price for being lucky enough to land a handsome, charming husband. She thought that men had to be babied. She protected my father and covered up for his errant ways. He was thoughtless, but he was the one we all adored. We let him off the hook. All of us married womanizers. My mother was resentful, though, and she took it out on us by being very critical, and raising us with a list of "shoulds." I dealt with the family problems by expressing my feelings, with the result that I was labeled as too sensitive, too selfish, and too emotional. In some ways, I was the most judged and the most lost. This judgmental attitude was still there when I pursued a successful professional career. In my mother's book, the worst thing that could happen to a woman was to be left alone. She would tell us that if we embarked on careers with men, we'd be alone in a man's world. She's the kind of woman who puts a lot of energy into pretending to be happy."

This is a vivid illustration of an unhealthy family system operating in response to the father's distance and to his drinking and womanizing. The mother endures her husband's behavior but takes out her resentment about it on her daughters. She raises them on a formula of "shoulds," and when any of her children violate the rules, parental judgments await them. Julie receives the stern-est judgments because she is the child who tries the hardest to assert her own individuality. Everybody dances around Dad, who is clearly the kingpin in the family, the person who has free rein to do whatever he pleases. He doesn't interfere with his wife's child-rearing practices, in fact, he absolves himself of parental responsibility. But despite his obvious irresponsibility and negligence, he comes out ahead. The whole family colludes in "letting him off the hook," and in so doing paves the way for the daughters to follow their mother's lead by marrying womanizers. In the end, the mother is the loser in her daughters' esteem. She receives the harshest sentence from them, not only because she has been the primary parent—the one who laid down the law and the one with whom most of their time was spent, but also because they mimic her negative qualities by marrying men like Dad.

Eventually, Julie's story has a happy ending. She re-linquishes her attachments to womanizers and finds a stable relationship with a reliable man. Her ability to triumph, in my opinion, has its antecedent in her girl-hood, when she showed herself to be the assertive, self-expressive child. One could say that she was born with the luck of the draw, with the right temperament to com-bat the pathology in the system. Now she can stand back and see her father for the very imperfect person that he was and, if not 100 percent forgiving of her mother, at least aware that she wasn't responsible for all the family problems.

Margaret, the younger of two daughters in another rigid family system in which the father was absent and dis-tant, shows us an interactional family pattern that is somewhat more role-bound than Julie's:

"My father was introverted. He loved us, but he didn't relate to us. He worked all the time. He was somewhat attentive when we were small, but the communication just wasn't there. He was so uninvolved in our lives that I can't think of any way that he influenced us, although I do see his influence on our choice of men. He was not a person to have fun with. My attraction to womanizers has a lot to do with the fun they offer. They're the opposite of my father. My mother was domineering, but she was remarkable too in that she was totally blind. Her handicap seemed to make her stronger. She tried to be positive and not to stress the negatives in life. She behaved independently, as if she didn't need my father at all. She was encouraging to the extent that she brought us up with the idea that we were marriageable. She thought that that was the role that girls should play in life. First you get a job; then you get married. She didn't let me go to college."

In this family, sex roles are locked in place. Father provides. Mother raises children. Daughters get ready for marriage. Here, the daughters' blame is distributed more equitably between the parents, giving mother a slightly more favorable edge.

Margaret did as she was told and married at eighteen in accordance with her mother's view that marriage was the big prize. She devoted herself to being a wife and mother while growing increasingly skeptical. Although she stuck it out in the marriage for fifteen years, midway through she began an affair with an older man. Thinking that perhaps she'd gone wrong by marrying a wild, immature teenager on her first go-around, she hoped that by becoming like her mother and attaching herself to a fatherly lover who was more reliable than her husband, she would bring order into her life. It was not to be. She divorced her husband and later became bored with her lover.

Throughout those years, she struggled constantly with "the good wife versus the emerging person conflict." Finally, she opted for the emerging person, and established herself in a promising career, but her romantic life since then has revolved around relationships with womanizers—the "fun" men.

"Stand by your man" was the message that Alice received from her mother, who didn't see much of her traveling businessman husband.

"My father was a good guy, but he was always absent. He wasn't involved in parenting me or my two older brothers. I didn't relate to him much. He was never around. My mother was very good to us. She was caring and nice. If she was resentful or depressed about my father's frequent absences, she never showed it. She put the best face on things. There were rewards for her, too. My father traveled a great deal all over the world, and she was able to accompany him on some of his trips. She would have liked me to marry right after college."

Now in her late thirties, Alice has not yet found a man to stand by. She relishes the entertaining and exciting company of womanizers, and although she maintains that she recognizes that they are long shots for marriage partners, she is still baffled by the fact that she has remained unmarried. Of all the women I interviewed, she appeared the one least disposed to connect past history with current romantic events. According to her, the relationship with her mother was a positive one. So far, however, she has been unable to convert the good identification with her mother into a good relationship with a man. It would be tempting to say, in her case, that the mysterious, distant father stands as the parent to be reckoned with, but from the time that I first met her, I had a feeling that Alice romanticized both parents. I asked whether she had ever harbored suspicions that her father was a womanizer or that her mother might have been depressed just below the surface. These questions jolted her, as if she had buried them somewhere in the depths of her psyche. To me she herself seemed depressed— just below the surface.

Karen's story of paternal distance and maternal depression was the most dramatic and tragic one I heard:

"I hardly saw my father. He was an alcoholic, and because he was drunk most of the time, he hardly related to me, my handicapped twin brother, or my older brother. My parents slept in separate rooms and wrote notes to each other when they had to communicate about something. He had an important job, and didn't spend much time at home. My mother was never mentally stable, but she got worse as time went on. She was so depressed that she stayed in her room for days on end. She didn't want to interact with us. Eventually, she was diagnosed as paranoid schizophrenic. Even though I hardly interacted with my father at all, my mother was jealous of me because she thought he liked me. When their marriage collapsed, she blamed me for it."

By the time she reached high school, Karen had become promiscuous. She began by involving herself in relationships with boys who had other girlfriends and then moved on to married men, most of whom had other women besides Karen and their wives. After the married-men sequence, Karen moved on to a series of relationships with alcoholics, several of whom were men from a lower socioeconomic background than her own; some of them were married, but all of them were womanizers. Along the way, she developed a drinking problem of her own, one that she has not completely conquered yet. At the age of thirty-eight, she's still unmarried, still choosing the wrong guys, and still wishing to be married. "I'd like one steady, devoted relationship with someone I can trust." When I responded that I didn't believe that was what she really wanted because she was doing everything possible to make sure it didn't happen, she replied, "Maybe I'm afraid of marriage, afraid that it's going to be a repeat of my parents' disaster."

Julie, Margaret, Alice, and Karen share certain biographical similarities. Their fathers were frequently absent from the home and were emotionally distant from their daughters when they were present. Two of the fathers were alcoholics. In all four families, the fathers had license to do as they pleased as long as they brought home the bacon. Julie's and Margaret's mothers *endured* their marriages, as did Alice's mother, although she apparently received more attention from her husband than the other two mothers did, so that she was less visibly depressed or resentful. From Karen's accounts, her mother caved in to depression early in the marriage and never regained any measure of mental stability.

Looking first at the effects of absentee-distant fathers on these four women, we can see that all of them later developed attachments to womanizers—men who were hard to pin down. These were fathers whose inattentiveness sabotaged their daughters' oedipal strivings. By being unavailable to their daughters, they robbed them of the opportunity to feel secure and confident about their femininity and their ability to be intimate with a man. As Dr. Appleton points out in his book, two of the consequences of growing up with a distant father are apt to be that the daughter either learns not to expect very much from men in the way of warmth, intimacy, closeness, and love, or she has an insatiable hunger for male attention which causes her to become addicted to the excitement of the courtship phase and dissatisfied with the characteristic lulls of long-lasting relationships.[2] I think that both of these consequences can operate simultaneously, that is, that the woman who doesn't expect much from a man can be the same woman who is addicted to the excitement of courtship. Womanizers, let us not forget, are men who offer little in the way of intimacy and plenty in the way of excitement.

Among twenty-four women in his study group who had distant relationships with their fathers, Dr. Appleton discovered that only three of them were able to improve on those relationships to create close bonds with husbands. Those three went out of their way to select men whose emotional availability was assured.[3]

Among the mothers in these families are two who endure their marriages—Julie's and Margaret's—one mother, Alice's, who gets some enjoyment from hers but makes no demands on her husband for parental participation, and one mother, Karen's, who is immobilized as a wife and mother. With the possible exception of Alice, none of the daughters has a female role model whose relationship with a man is fulfilling enough to be exemplary.

Deprived of the male-female testing ground that close father-daughter relationships provide and lacking positive feminine role models from mothers who are happy in their marital relationships, these daughters languish in unfulfilling liaisons with womanizers—men who are as emotionally distant as their fathers were. Julie, because she had an independent mind and a determined spirit, is the one patch of blue in this overcast sky.

Daddy's Girls and Mother's Rivals

Just as a father's distance sets the stage for his daughter's difficulties in love, so does the overbearing father contribute, in a different way, to his daughter's love ailments. Again, Dr. Appleton's thoughts are instructive:

Fathers who are too needful of the worship of their little girls, who are too disappointed in the real world and revel in this escape, cling too long, and try to stunt the growth and independence of their developing children, can bring up women who never leave psychologically. Some, when interviewed, are quite open about saying how none of their men measure up to their fathers, who are brighter, more considerate and better company.[4]

Although the women I interviewed were not as explicit about their continuing attachments to their overbearing or overinvolved fathers as some of Appleton's subjects were, evidence of incomplete separations from such fathers could be found between the lines. Jill is an example:

"Dad and I were close. I was the oldest of seven children. As far as he was concerned, I was supposed to be a boy and a concert pianist. Since I couldn't be a boy, he converted me into the little princess. He paid no attention to the other kids in the family. I did become a pianist. I was always seeing things through his eyes. I went to the college that he wanted me to attend, a renowned music school, and my first independent step came when I left that school in my twenties. He was very controlling, and was never really affectionate toward me. Eventually, he divorced my mother and married a younger woman. He was a womanizer."

When Jill was twenty-eight, she married a passive man. "I chose him because he was there, not because I was madly in love with him. I couldn't have been close to anybody at that point. I didn't have the capability." After the breakup of her marriage, Jill had several relationships with womanizers, each relationship accompanied by the fantasy that she would be secure and protected: "I will move in with one of them. He will set the stage. He will watch out for me. *It will be like coming home to Dad.*" If she were judged by appearances alone, Jill would look independent. She has a career and is self-supporting, but she says that she is not who she seems to be. "I'm very dependent. Remember, I was the special one, the talented one, the performer. I was doted on. I was even led to believe that I was morally superior to other people. Even now I get righteous sometimes. All the attention made me seem self-confident, but it was deceptive. Sometimes I think I'm a fake and that my successes don't mean anything."

Father is everywhere in Jill's adult story. In her choice of a husband, she mirrors herself in relation to her father. Her mate is as passive with her as she was with her father. She has no idea how to be close to a man, and as she moved into relationships with womanizers (men like her father), her fantasies about them were centered around protection. They would "set the stage" for her and take care of her just as her father had done. It would be just like "coming home to Dad." At mid-life she still struggles with dependency. It is hard for her to see herself as a competent, useful, and happy person or as someone who owns her successes and can take care of herself. She feels incomplete and suspects that she's an impostor. Take the sum total of all of her problems, and the answer will compute to the influence of her overbearing father who raised her to believe that her very existence depended on him. For her, men are lifelines rather than people. Her father is still very much with her.

The same can be said about Gloria, a beautiful brunette whose father was her first, lost love:

"My father was a big womanizer. He may have children I don't even know about. The night I was born he was with a woman. I was the youngest of six children. From infancy until I was eight years old, I was the apple of his eye. I loved him, was obsessed with him, worshiped him, and remember at age five being physically attracted to him and jealous of my mother. When I was eight or thereabouts he suddenly became as distant, mean, abusive, and critical toward me as he had been toward my siblings. From then on, we were never close. I stopped liking him. His message to me was: Try to please men, get to their hearts, do it through being attractive and sexual. To him, it was more important for a woman to have big boobs than to achieve anything in life."

Gloria has never married. Most of her relationships with men have been with womanizers. Once when she was twenty-eight, she met a warm, caring man. It was the first and only relationship she ever had that put her on equal terms with a man, but she could see that he wasn't going to become a prominent person or a huge success in life. "I passed him by *because I wanted to show my father that I could snag a successful man.* I had been taught that the only way to make it big in life was to attach yourself to a successful man. It's strange but true that I often find myself thinking, 'Gee, Dad would be happy to see me with this man or that man.' I'd like to be able to say to him, guess who likes me now. In my fantasy, my suitor would be some rich, famous man."

Gloria was Daddy's girl until he abandoned her. Had he remained as enmeshed with her as he was in her early years, it would undoubtedly have been difficult for her to find a man who could measure up to him, but as it was, she experienced a traumatic abandonment, the consequences of which are everywhere in evidence. Now nearing forty, this beautiful woman has spent twenty years searching for her lost father through her relationships with womanizers. "I can't make any demands on men," she explains, "because I'm too afraid I'll lose them if I do."

She's the kind of woman every womanizer wants. The fear of loss of love is ever-present in her mind. It has reduced her to thinking of herself as a bimbo in relationships with men, as a mere sex object. As a growing girl, she was a sex object to her father. Even his turning against her has sexual overtones, as if he were replacing sexual desire with physical abuse in order to escape the incestuous feelings he must have had for her. Thus, she has succumbed to allowing sexuality to be the glue that bonds her with men. "I don't think I could make a lasting relationship with a man. I would see it as my job to do that. I have no idea what it takes to keep somebody happy, and I wouldn't want any man to feel obligated to me."

Catherine has been a polio victim since she was one and a half years old. Throughout childhood and adolescence she wore leg braces and was subjected to constant abuse from peers. She is now a sweet, rather innocent-looking woman in her thirties, and the only vestige of her illness is discernible in a slight limp. When she was growing up, her father was her closest companion.

"I was my father's pet. He preferred me to my brother. I was more like him than my mother, so we were natural allies. He protected me, and was always good and understanding toward me. He never punished me. In general, though, he was kind of a boring person."

When it came time to marry, Catherine selected the least "boring" of her suitors. Rejecting her more reliable, steadier pursuers, she chose instead a twenty-six-year-old man she met "drag racing." Not only had he had a troubled childhood, but from adolescence into his twenties, he had lived a racy life with women, and he didn't let up during their courtship or after they were married. In addition, he was an alcoholic and physically abusive to Catherine. Finally, at age forty, he quit womanizing, drinking, and abusing, but by then Catherine had turned sour. At present, they merely coexist together. "I've stopped building my life around him. I've begun to have an independent life."

Catherine paid the price in her marriage for being the daughter of an overprotective, doting, lackluster father. "I never had any experience with independence when I was growing up. My father watched over me all the time. Now, I'm much more determined, but I'm just learning how to be independent. I married my husband because he was fun and adventurous. He would travel and do things. I'd never been anywhere, and I was sick to death of my dull life and the dull men I'd always known. He says he married me for my calmness." For Catherine, the mutual calmness that she shared with her father was the forerunner of her battle with boredom. Her husband's errant behavior may have spared her the boredom, but in place of adventure she received misery instead. By discouraging her from living as full a life as possible even with polio, her father contributed to her marital fate. Then, too, as a polio victim, she must have experienced severe psychological and physical pain, and without sufficient compensation in the form of fun and adventure, she had to have become accustomed to pain as a major fact of life. Thus, one might say that she was preconditioned for the marital misery she incurred.

All these Daddy's girls had mothers too. Jill's mother raised seven children without any help from her husband, who devoted what little emotional energy he had to Jill exclusively. Jill and her mother had no significant bonding until Jill was close to adolescence. Then her mother began to talk to her. Their relationship was more like a friendship than a mother-daughter connection.

"She would talk to me philosophically about boys, life, friendships, and my father's affairs with women. She was totally permissive. There were no rules. Around the time that she began to relate to me, she also began drinking. Although I think she cared about me, she was an ineffectual parent."

Gloria decided early in her life that she had to do everything possible to avoid being like her mother.

"My mother was a typical German hausfrau and nothing more. She was semi-illiterate and never stood up to my father. She never protected us from his abuse, and she herself was abused by him."

Catherine's mother was much less passive than Jill's or Gloria's. She was someone who demanded obedience, and thus invited the rebelliousness her daughter demonstrated by her choice of a husband.

"My mother was stern. You had to follow the rules. I went along with her until I picked my husband. She was rigid, domineering, and controlling."

Even a cursory reading of these mother-daughter relationships drives home the point that there were no positive, maternal role models for these daughters. Jill's oedipal rivalry with mother was *aborted* by mother's passivity so that she was given no opportunity to compete for and lose her father's affection. First, she tried to gain a connection to her mother and to her own femininity by marrying someone passive like her mother. Having failed in that endeavor, her relationships with womanizers can be viewed as her attempt to restage the oedipal drama, to reenact a rivalry with mother so that she emerges as the loser and avails herself of the opportunity to redefine her femininity. She entered into liaisons with the kind of men who placed her in triangular patterns with them and their other women, patterns that *guaranteed that she would eventually lose the men's affections.*

For Jill the move from the marriage to the womanizers represents a progression of sorts, since she moved from a pre-oedipal dyad (as symbolized by the marriage to her motherlike husband) to an oedipal triad (herself, a man, and another woman), but it stopped short of securing her the positive female identification that she needed to fashion a mature relationship with a man. Since she is an oedipally fixated adult, every loss of a love relationship does damage to her self-esteem.

Gloria's oedipal struggle was first *aborted* by her mother's passivity and later *sabotaged* by her father's cruel rejection of her. By the time she reached adulthood, she was like a ship lost at sea. With conscious intent to be different from her mother and with deep wounds from her father's abandonment, she left home at age nineteen without any of the psychological reserves she needed to help her find her own way in the world. She drifted from one man to another or, more accurately, from one caretaker to another.

Her story speaks to survival rather than to the enjoyment of living. It is a pre-oedipal story. Like the infant who needs the mother's physical nurturance to thrive, Gloria needs men for the same purpose. She can't ask for anything, and she can't offer happiness to anyone. All she can do is be grateful for whatever she gets, and she doesn't get much. She doesn't even put up a fight against the other women in the lives of the womanizers she attracts. There are no demands, no strings attached. Instead, she accepts her second-class status, is appreciative of the little bonuses it affords her. The cruel irony of it all is that the harder she has tried to distance herself from identification with her mother, the closer she comes to resembling her. Although replacing her mother's

"hausfrau" image with her own more glamorous de-
meanor, Gloria, like her mother before her, is a symbol
of female servitude to men.

Not so with Catherine. She is a fighter, first against
polio, second against her mother, and third against her
husband. Although she doesn't say so, there is some suggestion in her characterization of her relationship with
her mother of an *exaggerated* oedipal rivalry between
mother and daughter. Toward her daughter, the mother
is "rigid, domineering, and controlling," and while we
can't be certain that the mother's sternness toward Catherine is inspired by jealousy of Catherine's relationship
with her father, we are entitled to harbor suspicions to
that effect. Certainly, Catherine's choice of a husband is
grist for this interpretive mill. Rather than select a "boring" partner as her mother did, thereby identifying with
her mother, Catherine heads in the opposite direction.
She chooses the one man who is least palatable to her
mother as a son-in-law, and in doing so she perpetuates
the mother-daughter rivalry. The battle opponents are
then expanded in Catherine's marriage to include her
husband's other women. Eventually, as we are presum-
ing occurred in relation to her father, Catherine triumphs.
Not only did she win the competition with her mother
for her father's affection, but she also wins the rounds
with her husband's women. He stops womanizing, but,
alas, victory at the front door brings defeat through the
back door. For a daughter, winning the oedipal contest
is tantamount to losing it. The successful outcome of the
struggle requires the mother to win her man and the
daughter to give him up in order to pave the way for
following her mother's positive example in her adult love
choice. After winning back her husband, Catherine discovers that she no longer cares for him. He is no better
suited to the role of her Mr. Right than her father was.
And still her mother's example holds no hope for her

romantic future. As she says, "If I had it to do over again, I'd never get married."

Cruelty and Criticism— Oppressive Fathers and Mothers

Some of the daughters I talked to appeared to have *fought their way through childhood,* attempting as best they could to defend themselves against parental oppression. Others seemed to have *succumbed* to it. Whichever route they took, they entered adulthood devoid of much, if any, experience with harmonious parent-child interactions. They were overexposed to the uses and abuses of parental power, and whether they struggled against or yielded to it, they would later come to imbue their romantic relationships with the emblems of power rather than love.

Frances was one of the daughters who surrendered to her parents.

"My father was committed to the family, but he was extremely critical and nurtured high expectations for his five children, especially for me and my brother as the two oldest. He was joined in his critical attitude by my mother, who, in addition to being critical, was cold and unaffectionate. She never kissed me or told me she loved me. She was a martyr who never asked for anything from my father and didn't get much in the way of support or encouragement from him. My father was somewhat more affectionate than she was, but his affection had an aggressive, physical quality which bordered on being abusive. I was wary of him. He was a drinker as well, and I suspect that he was a woman-izer. On the whole, he didn't relate much to me. He was distant most of the time, but when he did relate it was with criticism. The essence of living with my parents was that you knew you could never please them, so why bother to try."

Here is the distant father and the depressed, martyred mother again, but on top of those deficits is the couple's collusion in scapegoating their children, a practice that undoubtedly served as an outlet for their marital frustrations. Frances determined that it was a "no win" situation to try to obtain their affection and approval. She abandoned the struggle. At twenty-one she married and played the same tape all over again. From the starting gate to the finish of the marriage, her husband woman-ized. Aside from confronting him about his affairs and initiating one short round of marriage counseling, Frances did little else but devote herself to her man in the hope that she could hang on to him. Again, she lost.

She was the classic "doormat" wife. In addition to being unfaithful, her husband was abusive to her and intermit-tently to their children, but still she remained loyal and devoted. "All he wanted was power and control," she said, "and I couldn't let him go. I loved him and I loved being married." The only kind of "love" that Frances knew anything about was the bonding that exists be-tween victimizer and victim. That was her definition of love.

Claire was more combative in her family than Frances was. The two families share a certain thread of common-ality. Like Frances, Claire was one of five children born to a depressed, martyred mother and a "moderately al-coholic" father. Claire's father, however, was as cruel as he was critical. He endowed his daughter with a fear of men.

"I was one of five children. I was my father's favorite even though we fought constantly. He didn't like my independent spirit. He was a moderate alcoholic. Although he didn't do that much for me and actually abused me physically on several occasions, my mother was jealous of me for what he did do, as were my siblings. My mother was depressed, but spent her adult life catering to my father and working hard as a homemaker. Her two brothers were alcoholics and my two brothers are alcoholics. One of my sisters was sexually abused by one of my brothers. My father frequently beat my brothers, but my mother never protected any of us from each other or from our father. She denied all the perverse behavior that was going on."

As a result of her life with her father, Claire has positioned herself in a permanent Catch-22 with men. Married in her early twenties to a man who began pursuing other women (some of whom had been good friends of hers) as soon as she became pregnant with her first child, she was determined to prevent her husband's cruelty from consuming her. One and a half years after the birth of their child, her husband left her. "There wasn't room for two babies in the house." She joined women's groups, enrolled in graduate school, and busied herself caring for her infant son, showing the same independent spirit she had exhibited toward her father.

Underneath the exterior spunk, there were interior wounds left over from her husband's abandonment. After her marriage, all of the other meaningful relationships in her life have been with men who have been abusive to her or men who have been womanizers like her husband. She can't get off the track even though she understands why she's stuck on it.

"My father believed that because he had suffered, his children should suffer too. He was cruel, but I wanted

to win him. He died before I could finish my fight with
him. He made me fearful of men, but paradoxically it
is powerful, attractive men with no ability to be caring
whom I seek out. They're men just like him. With every
new man, I tell myself that I'm going to win on this
round, but of course I never do."

Claire, in sum, has spent most of her life attempting to
conquer men, and this has required that she commit herself wholeheartedly to romantic battle rather than to romantic bliss.

Susan was the combatant in her family too. Her father
was strict, the ruler in the family. If his children didn't
behave as he wanted them to, he hit them. "He may have
been a little more lenient toward me than toward my
brothers, because I was a girl, but it was a matter of degree." Susan's mother was her husband's faithful assis-
tant. She, too, wanted her children to behave by the book,
and in her book it was important to be conventional and
fashionable. Both parents wanted Susan to grow into a
"respectable" young lady. Susan didn't toe the line.

"I was tall and lanky. I didn't date much in high school
or college. After college I was a dancer in New York,
and I got involved in macrobiotics. My husband and I
met through macrobiotics. At one point in our lives we
had both been craftspeople so we had that in common
too. Otherwise we were very different. He was older
than I was and shorter. He had a foreign background,
spoke many languages, and swept me off my feet, off
to Europe and into marriage. We had a kind of honeymoon existence until after our first baby was born. Then
he began seeing other women on a regular basis. He
felt he was entitled to these relationships and to the
home base that I provided for him. I challenged him
on all of this. There were several separations and rec-
onciliations which went on for nine years. After the
second baby, I told him to go."

"I'm a bit rebellious," says Susan, "you might say I was anti-Daddy." She's right. I did say that and said that she was anti-Mommy too. "I guess I like to go against the tide," she added. Her major weapon in the struggle against her parents was her romantic nature. Looking back on her marriage, she sees it as accidental, as something she fell into rather than sought. "I'm not a dependent type. I was capable of living just as well without a man as with one," she maintains.

The observer, however, could view her marriage as evidence that she had simply found a new forum for an old fight. She married a man who, like her father, played by his rules and expected her to follow suit. Again, she disobeyed. Her marriage bore no resemblance to her mother's vision of respectability, and yet with her own children, Susan is revealing herself to be cut from her mother's cloth. "I am strict, exact, and particular with my kids, especially about their health-food diet. There's no cheating permitted."

Susan, so it would seem, fights power with her own brand of power. For her the thrill of relationships seems to lie in the stimulating intensity of the ongoing power struggle. It matters not whether she is the conqueror or the conquered. She calls herself "naïve," and says that naïveté led her into the accidental marriage, but she is naïve only about love, not about power, and the truth is that the more she learns about power, the less she will learn about love.

Sylvia, who is nearing fifty, knows nothing about love. How could she? Both her parents abused her physically, and her mother abused her sexually before she was five years old.

"I got no affection and no kisses. Whatever I did wasn't good enough. I had an older sister and she was the perfect daughter in my parents' eyes. Anything I got from them I had to beg for. I had no allies in the family except for my mother's father. He did care for me. I visited him in the summer. He was good to me. I was a great student, an all-around teenager who excelled in sports, studies, and any number of hobbies. I got college scholarships, but my parents wouldn't let me go. The day I graduated from high school I left home and made my way in the world."

By the age of twenty-two, Sylvia was a married woman, and one and a half years later, after seven hospitalizations necessitated by her husband's persistent battering of her, she mustered the strength to kick her husband out of the house. From that day until a later time when she settled in one locality and into a career, her story was one of hand-to-mouth survival played out in a variety of geographic settings. Sylvia never remarried, but she was engaged thirteen times. Her romantic life has been a revolving door of short-term flings with men, all of whom were womanizers and most of whom were rich.

"Womanizers are the only men who interest me. Other types bore me to death. Womanizers have money. Thanks to them I have beautiful jewelry and great clothes, and I've been able to travel far and wide and dine at great restaurants. They're terrific in bed. I'm addicted to them."

Among the women I interviewed, Sylvia was the purest love addict. Her addiction to womanizers was *ego-syntonic*, which is to say that it was nonconflictual for her. Womanizers gave her exactly what she wanted— material and sexual comforts without the burden of long-lasting commitment. When one left her, there was always another one to take his place. Having no conception of a kind of love that transcends the boundaries of personal neediness, she gave of herself for the sole purpose of receiving favors from men. This is the precise formula required for power-playing and the most antithetical to loving. Sylvia is a woman who gives with a singular purpose—to guarantee a good return. "I get taken care of, but I nurture too in order to keep this type of man for as long as I want him."

The establishment of family triangles that pit parents against one or more of their children is a common method that many disaffected couples employ to diffuse marital conflict. In her popular book *Intimate Partners,* author Maggie Scarf describes how and why these triangles are set in place:

> Emotional triangles come into being because they offer a disaffected and distressed couple a way of *not* confronting the problems and disappointments that one or both of them are simply too scared to think about, much less talk about openly. By enlarging the conflict in such a way that *three* people are involved, the tensions in the relationship can often be successfully obscured from every one of the people involved. And while getting into a triangle inevitably commits the pair to a series of endlessly repeated skirmishes, it helps them stave off the all-out battle which might well end in the total defeat of one of them or the destruction of the emotional system itself.[5]

The kind of emotional triangle which positions the child as *the odd one out* is the type that Frances, Claire, Susan, and Sylvia experienced. As Scarf goes on to say:

> . . . the marital partners are able to unite around the problems they are having with their "bad," incorrigible child. In this sort of circumstance, familiar to most therapists, the couple usually sees themselves as lovingly in unison; they have no difficulties aside from

the ones that they are having with their unmanageable offspring.[6]

Although the parents of these four women did not, in every instance, appear "lovingly in unison," they weren't divorced and they did unite in the critical or abusive treatment they gave their daughters. The net effect of the triangulation was, as we have seen, the daughters' propensity to become *weak victims* or *strong combatants*. Later, in their adult love relationships, they would replay these predesignated roles, and would invariably choose men whose behavior toward them made it easy to slip back into the familiar part.

Daughters who have had to endure long-standing adversarial relationships with *both* their parents are ripe candidates to serve as sparring partners or "whipping girls" to power-driven men. On a conscious level, they wish only to be loved, but on an unconscious level, they are programmed for a power struggle. And, as my family therapy mentors used to reiterate to their students, "As soon as *power* comes in the door, any chance for *intimacy* goes out the door."

If a woman becomes conditioned either to victimization or to combat, it is hard for her to find alternative ways of relating. As the victim, she assumes from the start that she is the weaker party in a relationship, and in some measure she welcomes this position since it absolves her from taking adult responsibility to determine the eventual course of the relationship. From her point of view, whatever happens between her and her mate, is *his* doing, not *hers*. The combatant, on the other hand, is driven by the intensity, vibrancy, and suspense that accompany power struggles and elude more tranquil interactions. When combative women speak of certain men as *boring*, they frequently mean that they're not the type they can wrangle with. Wrangling is more stimulating

for many women than loving is, just as war is more stimulating for many militarists than peacetime is. The
best wranglers are the women who were trained from an
early age.

Another way of exercising power and staving off intimacy in a relationship is illustrated by Sylvia's example.
No need for her to engage in direct combat with men.
She operates by a simple code: *power-playing*. The im-
plicit, unspoken agreement is that she will give men what
they want—sex, nurturance, and companionship—in return for what she wants—clothes, travel, restaurants, and
jewelry. When she and/or her partner have had their fill,
either one or both of them is free to break up the partnership. In her relationships with men, she functions as
a coequal, a woman who makes sure that the balance of
power never tips in favor of the man. Thus, intimacy is
replaced by commerce, *her* services for *his* goods, without requirements for knowing one another or caring about
each other.

It goes almost without saying that for Frances, Claire,
Susan, and Sylvia there are no mothers who serve as
positive, feminine role models and no endearing oedipal
fathers to love and lose. While I cannot state it as fact, I
came away from my meetings with the four of them with
the impression that they continued to be more troubled
by their relationships with their fathers than with their
mothers, and more inclined in adulthood to seek emotional resolutions with their fathers. It was as if they were
saying, "Mom was the way she was, and that's that, but
I can't accept that Dad was the way he was. I need some
form of redress from him."

As evidence for this point of view, I offer the following biographical examples: Frances married the carbon
copy of her father, and didn't want to give him up despite all his cruelty to her. Claire stated openly that she
was still trying to win her father through her relation-

ships with men who reminded her of him. Susan found
the autocratic match for her father in her husband, and a
career for herself that is similar to her father's, both
choices suggesting that gaining her father's approval has
been more important to her than the receipt of a maternal seal of approval. Sylvia, treated as abusively by her
father as by her mother throughout her childhood, returned in mid-life to make peace with him, but has not
done so with her mother.

If there is an inference to be drawn from these snip-
pets, it would surely have to be that women regard their
relationships with men as matters of paramount importance, and they begin to do so at a fairly early age. I was
forced to confront this reality when our sixteen-year-old
daughter was left heartbroken by a boyfriend who broke
up with her. Her thirteen-year-old sister, having wit-
nessed her older sister's anguish for many days, finally
said one day in total frustration and bewilderment, "Mom,
you'd think Amy had been married, the way she's carry-
ing on!"

Whether married or single, women do "carry on" about
men, and this is not especially good news for woman-
kind, because it implies that if given the choice between
our own self-development and a relationship with a man,
we will usually opt for the latter. Having lost respect for
our mothers for "selling out" to our fathers, some of us
proceed to repeat the mistake in our own love lives and
then suffer the consequence in the loss of self-reliance.
Way down deep, behind the voices of love-torn women,
I think I hear a plea for female leadership which sounds
something like this:

"Show us how to love men and be all that we can be
at the same time. Teach us how to acquire enough individual self-worth to overcome our fear of male abandonment and our dependency on men. Lead us into

loving men as one piece of life's joy rather than the whole of it."

Loss of a Parent— Daughters in Grief

Three of the women I interviewed had experienced the death of a parent in their childhoods, and they spoke openly about the effect of these losses on their later relationships with men.

Sara's father died suddenly when she was ten years old. She was an only child, and her father had been, in her words, "warm, adoring, and encouraging. He enjoyed and valued me, and he wanted me to achieve."

"My father's death was the pivotal experience of my life. It took me twenty years to deal with it. It happened so suddenly that there was no way to say good-bye. I wasn't allowed to go to the funeral. I didn't believe that he was really dead. I kept on having a relationship with him."

Sara's father's death occurred between the Kennedy and King assassinations. "It was an uncertain world for me. I became distrustful. These feelings carried over to adulthood. I felt I couldn't count on permanency with a man. I insisted on financial independence and wouldn't let a man support me. I wanted to be self-reliant." Sara, in her choice of lovers, did everything possible to prevent permanency. Aside from a brief marriage to a faithful but emotionally unstable man, she spent most of her twenties and part of her thirties in relationships with womanizers. By the time she reached thirty-five, she had changed her mind about permanency—twenty-five years after her father's death. Finally, then, she could allow herself to entertain the thought of "happily ever after," and fortunately, she met someone with whom it could be possible. In a moment combined with irony and humor, she shared a current fantasy with me: "I'd like to be locked in a room with a man for one hundred years. Someone would knock at the door, and we'd both say we're not done yet."

Laura lost her mother when she was fifteen. Until her death, Laura's mother had been the mainstay of the family, the one who provided all the care and nurturance. Laura's father was the distant kind, who spent long hours at his job and gave little of himself to his children. He was a "problem person," a drinker and a man given to outbursts of temper. When Laura reached adolescence, he became the sole parent, and he handled his role by being excessively strict with his children. Laura was not allowed to date, was forced into the role of surrogate mother to her younger siblings, and was cut off from long-standing, happy relationships with her mother's relatives as the result of her father's fear that they would threaten his own hold on his children. All of the fun, intimacy, and warmth in Laura's life vanished with her mother's death. Even grief was not permitted.

Laura's entrance to college coincided with her father's remarriage. Finally, she gained a measure of independence which was matched by a determination to make up for all the fun she had missed earlier. She was drawn to the "good-time guys," to the kind of men her father would call "sinners." By twenty-three, she was married.

"I chose my husband because he was *fun*. He was charming and active. On the surface, he seemed cheerful and sweet. He offered to buy me the world, and would go out of his way to please me. He married me because I was wifely, my intelligence was an asset to his business, and, most importantly, because I wasn't assertive enough to stand in his way. He knew that I would do everything I could to accommodate and please him. He was the biggest "good time guy" of any I had met. I can't count the number of affairs he had while we were married. Most of them were with young, sleazy women who worked for him. For him, life was one big party after another. He told me once that he had to have sex every five minutes, and since I wasn't fulfilling his needs adequately, he had to womanize. My "fun" mate turned out to be a misogynist, a man with a vendetta against a vicious mother who had demanded that he be the all-adoring son. He womanized because he *had* to hurt women. I hung in with him for ten years, because I was terrified of losing another family. A family was all I'd ever wanted."

Now Laura is a thirty-three-year-old single mother of two children. Whatever "fun" she had was short-lived, and worse still, she relost a family. Taken by itself, the loss of Laura's misogynist husband is a positive event in her life, a sign of her personal strength, but the fact that she married him in the first place subjected her to a more significant loss—the loss of the *ideal* of the intact family. Had she been allowed to grieve over her mother's death, she might have avoided the need to place herself in a situation that came with a *guarantee* of loss. These days, Laura plays it safe. "I'm not dating now. I want to be sure that I can take care of myself, and before I get hooked up with someone else, I want to be rid of any leftover anger and baggage. I don't think I know yet what a normal man is like. I have no role models."

Elizabeth, a woman in her sixties, knew even less than Laura did about what a normal man was like. She was thirteen when her father died, but she had very little contact with him from the time that she was ten, when her mother died. Shortly thereafter her father became ill, and she was sent from her home with him to another state where she resided with an aunt and uncle. After that she lived with a series of aunts. At age thirteen, around the time of her father's death, she was sent to boarding school.

"I was an only child. My father was a happy drunk, a once-a-year binger. I adored him. He was very gregarious. He'd been a vaudeville actor, and he used to take me to the theater with him. I was his little darling. He was fun. My mother was a wonderful woman. I loved her dearly, but from the time she became ill when I was nine, I saw very little of her, and then she was gone."

In the space of a year, Elizabeth's world fell apart, and by the time she was thirteen, both her parents were dead. With the reservoir of pain that Elizabeth brought to adolescence, it was inevitable that she, like Laura, would be attracted to the "fun" men. She became a party girl, and gravitated instinctively toward the party boys. At eighteen, she was married to one of them, a "popular Andy Hardy, Mickey Rooney type who loved the girls and was loads of fun." By age nineteen, she was tired of married life and was back on the party circuit. Her second husband came on the scene when she was twenty-one. He was tall, blond, and handsome, and within six days of their meeting, they were married. Their rocky marriage lasted for thirty-three years, but throughout that time they never really settled down. Essentially, their marriage was an extended party. Two children were born, but their father was no more committed to parenting than he was to husbanding. He had numerous affairs, most of which Elizabeth accepted or chose to overlook. An increasing distance developed between them until finally, when he reached mid-life, he divorced Elizabeth to marry his young secretary.

Divorce was frightening for Elizabeth. She was nervous. Her doctor prescribed Valium and Librium, and neglected to tell her that these combined with alcohol consumption could be dangerous. Over fifty and alone, Elizabeth became a problem drinker.

One can look at Elizabeth's life from early adolescence on as a saga of pain avoidance. The traumatic loss of both her parents and the lack of stable family ties thereafter prevented her from managing or confronting pain again. Her life has been a kind of living death in which she appears to have been carried along by events— things happening *to* her. She has never been the mistress of her destiny.

In Summary

In this chapter, we have seen that the quality of a daughter's adult relationships with men is determined to a great extent by the kind of connection she had to each of her parents.

Fathers give daughters their first exposure to men, and the way that Dad treats his little girl has a long-standing effect on her feminine identity and self-confidence. While most modern women are aware that their relationships with their fathers affect their later romantic fortunes, they often sidestep this awareness and allow themselves to be swept away by the excitement and intensity of misguided love affairs. Thus they subject themselves to painful love experiences which could be avoided if they kept their knowledge about their relationships with their fathers in the forefront of their minds.

In addition, many women are prone to allow men too much power in a relationship, thereby permitting more maltreatment than they should. This tendency can be attributed, in part, to the attitudes about women's status vis-à-vis men that prevailed before women's liberation had a significant impact on society—attitudes that were hard to shed despite progress toward first-class citizenship for women. Among the fathers of women involved with womanizers, there was a persistent pattern of misuse or abuse of paternal power, and as the case examples illustrate, it left its mark on all the daughters.

Generally, the mothers of the women I interviewed were perceived by their daughters as inadequate feminine role models, and often received more blame for their daughters' adult discontent than the fathers did, even in instances where the father was clearly the more negligent of the two parents. While it was evident that maternal examples did have a bearing on the daughters' love lives, the respondents tended to be more preoccupied throughout adulthood with rehashing the father-daughter dyad than the mother-daughter dyad. In part, this is because women view male-female relationships as more vital to personal happiness than female-female relationships.

The family systems of the female interviewees were characterized by rigid role definitions, and many references were made to the fallout that resulted from the lack of elasticity in the family interactions. In one family the fallout was that all the daughters married womanizers.

The four categories of marital dysfunction that were most prevalent among women who loved womanizers were: 1. Distant Fathers—Depressed or Martyred Mothers; 2. Daddy's Girls and Mother's Rivals; 3. Oppressive Fathers and Mothers; 4. Parental Loss.

In the first category—women with distant fathers and depressed mothers—the adult daughters had great difficulty forming close bonds with men. Their relationships with womanizers tended to perpetuate the distant connections they had had with their fathers, and their mothers served as negative role models for them in relation to men.

The Daddy's girls had difficulty separating from their fathers. Their fathers haunted them in adulthood so that they became excessively dependent on men for their self-esteem. They were prone to select womanizers who served as father figures for them. This group of women were vocal in their disdain for their mothers. Mothers were either background figures or objects of contempt.

Daughters of critical and/or oppressive parents tended to become either *victims* or *combatants* in their relationships with womanizers. These stances were often continuations of childhood postures that they had assumed in order to cope with parental mistreatment. Among this group of women, there were indications that they were more troubled in adult life by their unresolved relationships with their fathers than by those with their mothers.

The women who had experienced the death of a parent(s) in early childhood all showed some vestige of their loss in later relationships with men. Either they were afraid of permanency with a man and thus selected womanizers as a way of avoiding it, or they sought to circumvent the pain of the original loss through their connections to "fun" womanizers—men with whom they imagined they would feel no pain. Eventually, these relationships proved extremely painful and reintroduced them to loss. For some women, the loss of the womanizer(s) was a liberating experience, which freed them at last from debilitating pain avoidance.

CHAPTER III

Don't Fence Us In

When I asked men why they womanized, I received a variety of answers. Some were simple: "It's pleasant." "I love women." Others were complex: "I think it's because I lack self-worth." "I do it because I have more sexual energy than any one woman could tolerate." As a psychotherapist by profession, I had my own ideas about why they did it, so I was curious to see whether my hunches correlated with their statements. For the most part they didn't, but that didn't make their answers less valid or interesting to me. What you are about to read, then, is a composite of "expert" opinion: theirs, mine, and that of other writers. Although I often thought that my subjects were unconsciously rationalizing their motives for womanizing, I never doubted that they were giving me explanations that they believed to be true. Their answers fell under three general headings.

Freedom

Americans are proud of their individual freedoms. Freedom, American-style, is as much a psychological concept as a political one. One of our most cherished freedoms is the freedom to pursue our personal happiness. We want what we want when we want it and as consumers of happiness we don't have much talent for postponing gratification. Buying now and paying later, a concept that began as an advertising slogan, has evolved into a national habit. The problem with it, though, is that eventually it leads to the discovery that having it all contributes more toward stimulating rather than satisfying our collective appetite for happiness. It can lead us on a perpetual search for "more" and "better." As freedom lovers, we don't want anybody standing in our way, whether "anybody" be governments, institutions, authorities, spouses, or other individuals.

From the womanizers who confided in me, I came to see the practice of womanizing as one reflection in the large American freedom mirror. Womanizers are men who place extraordinary value on individual freedom. They are men who have oversized appetites for personal happiness and fulfillment. They want women when they want them and, as will become evident, they have abundant energy to apply to the quest. One man, age forty-one, a bachelor who had been married very briefly when he was nineteen, put it in perfect perspective:

"I've been chasing women for all of my adult life. Once in a while I'd click into one person for six months to two years, but I never could be truly monogamous. I can't live up to the American standard of monogamy.

I'd have to live in a country where I'd have societal permission to have affairs. Ironically, if I were to make a move like this, I think I'd probably be faithful to one person because the freedom to be unfaithful would be granted to me."

There are countries where womanizing is an acceptable behavior for married men. Susan Trausch, in an article in *The Boston Globe* following the Gary Hart affair, had this to say about Italy:

A woman I know who went to Italy last summer tells the story of her relatives being absolutely amazed that Americans were in such a swivet over former presidential candidate Gary Hart's fling with model Donna Rice. After all, everybody has affairs in the old country, and the American visitor was considered strange for having a long-time "significant other" instead of a husband. Italians see no irony in supporting marriage and family while supporting extramarital affairs. That's simply the way life is and has been for thousands of years, so why sweat it?[1]

In America, we do sweat about womanizing. For many years, we tolerated, admired, and disapproved of it at the same time. More recently, due to a strong push from women, we have become less tolerant of it and more vocal about our disapproval. In times past, we made a distinction between single womanizers and married womanizers in that the former did not risk the loss of society's seal of approval. Now, however, while the average citizen may not frown upon the bachelor womanizer, the professional mental-health establishment looks upon him with equal suspicion. Labels have been coined to describe him. Like his married counterpart, he is called a "commitmentphobic," a "love-addict," or a "narcissistic character type." From the expert-opinion perspec-

tive, the bachelor womanizer and the married womanizer
are alike in that they both lack the psychic capability to
sustain a loving relationship with a woman. Once expert
opinion reaches a large public audience, it becomes
popular parlance, and social pressure begins to mount.
So the social tides are turning against womanizers regardless of marital status.

Some of the men I interviewed spoke of themselves as
former womanizers. They referred, sometimes nostalgi-
cally, to the era of the sixties and seventies when society
seemed to be favorably disposed toward sexual promiscuity, the word "womanizer" was rarely heard, and when
it was it didn't carry the taint of disapproval that it does
now. A man in his mid-forties told me:

> "I was in my late twenties and early thirties when I
> did most of my womanizing. It was fun then. Every-
> body was doing it. It was typical and conventional.
> Those of us who jumped on the bandwagon liked our-
> selves a lot. We were proud of our attractiveness to
> women and totally insensitive to the potential for any
> emotional wreckage that might result from our behav-
> ior. We were free to experiment, and we took full ad-
> vantage of the freedom. Even though I'm still
> unmarried, I couldn't carry on with women now the
> way I did then. The social stigma against it is too
> strong."

In the free-spirited sixties and seventies, men could
more easily justify their womanizing behavior on the
grounds that women were enjoying the same sexual freedoms that men were. Thus, men could sidestep the ex-
ploitation issue. If women were choosing to be
promiscuous because sexual liberation had been awarded
to them, then how could men be accused of taking advantage of women? One of the major problems with this
line of reasoning was its disregard for the fact that what-

ever had been gained by way of sexual parity had not been matched by economic parity. Despite all the sexual romping and the liberation marching, women were still not receiving equal pay for equal work. They still needed men for financial support.

Added to the economic reality was another fundamental truth. Political action didn't prevent people of both sexes from falling in love with one or another of their lovers, or from being hurt by the dissolution of romantic entanglements. If the wounded party was a woman and her lover a womanizer, there had to be emotional wreckage no matter how permissive or condoning society was about womanizing. For one of the most disturbing symbols of the era and of the wreckage from womanizing, one needs only to recall Marilyn Monroe's suicide.

The pursuit of personal happiness seems, then, to be a double-edged freedom. It's nice to be able to do what you want and get what you want when you want it, but there's always this potential for wreckage that accompanies the freedom, whether we're talking about womanizers or other habitual happiness seekers. If one's personal happiness comes at the expense of someone else's happiness, the price can be too high. The historian Lawrence Stone has said that when individualism predominated over the interests of the kin group in Western culture, men and women were left free to decide on marital partners without parental or familial intervention. As a consequence, Stone says:

Today individualism is given such absolute priority in most Western societies that couples are free to act as they please, to sleep with whom they please, to marry and divorce when and whom they please, to suit their own pleasure. The psychic cost of such behavior and its self-defeating consequences are becoming clear, however, and how long this situation will last is anybody's guess.[2]

In my discussions with the "freedom-loving" sample of womanizing men, they frequently referred to this moral and/or psychic dilemma. Some of them handled it by stating at the outset of every romantic encounter that the relationship would have no long-term potential. Others would stall until they had a reading of a woman's feelings. If she seemed headed in the direction of deeper involvement, this kind of man would terminate the relationship before the woman reached the passionate-attachment stage. In a few instances, the men said that their habit was to stand by until the woman ended the affair—usually when she recognized that it was going nowhere. In this scenario, some men reported feeling guilty for having let things go too far and hurting their partners. Despite their acknowledgment of the moral dilemma, the majority of the men I interviewed did not use it as a basis for ceasing the practice of womanizing. Instead, they would create new strategies designed to prevent or diminish the pain of separation. Those men who did decide to stop womanizing did so for other reasons. The point to be emphasized here is that while many womanizers expressed regret and guilt about the heartbreak their behavior may have caused, rarely did it serve as an impetus to alter the behavior.

Sex

There is one refrain that echoes through every conversation with a womanizer. Like a group marching for a cause, they have a slogan: "PLEASE UNDERSTAND," they declare, "THAT WE ARE MEN WHO ARE BLESSED WITH MORE SEXUALITY AND SEXUAL

ENERGY THAN THE MAJORITY OF OUR BRETH-
REN." Where one man bemoans it, another accepts it,
and where one man is proud of it, another is philosoph-
ical about it. The bemoaner says:

"I'm married now, and I've made a vow of monogamy,
but I have to be very careful because I'm easily lured
by women. Luckily, my work keeps me relatively iso-
lated. I need isolation in order to avoid the tempta-
tions of the flesh. My sexual energy is very high."

The accepting man says:

"Womanizing is a way of life. I want a lot of sex. I'm a
member of a male pack, all of whom are womanizers
or want to be. I don't feel guilty about it."

The proud man says:

"I love the variety of sexual experiences that womanizing offers. Each one is a challenge, and I love to win."

The philosopher says:

"Womanizing is out of my control. I believe that my
instinctual qualities are stronger than my intellectual
qualities. I agree with Toffler who says we're all basi-
cally animals. Men are drawn first by the visual and
only secondarily to the protector role. I don't womanize with the intention of hurting anyone."

Another philosopher says:

"I think a lot of men go to college, get married, and go
about their business. Sex isn't very important to them
or to their wives. They kind of fit it in. These are men

who aren't very aware of women. They have underdeveloped aesthetic and sexual senses."

In one way or another all of these men are saying that there's not too much they can or should do about their hypersexuality. Short of self-enforced seclusion from temptation, the individual is left to the mercy of a biological imperative. Accompanying the biological fatalism is an attitude of pride in one's virility. There are no hints that anyone would prefer a less sexualized existence. From what they tell me, I have the impression that many womanizers are diligent locker-room researchers. They talk to monogamous married men regularly, and invariably they come away from their informal surveys with fresh evidence that their subjects are a sexually disgruntled lot.

Womanizers, according to their own theory, then, are men who are simply doing what comes naturally. They don't repress their sexuality nor silence it with guilt. It's God-given and intended to be used.

Experts abound to take aim at this sexual-energy theory. One of the most comprehensive attacks comes from theologian William May in a contributing chapter to the book *Passionate Attachments*. May names and describes four conflicting theories of sex: The Demonic, The Divine, The Casual, and The Nuisance. He declares all of them "mischievous." The Casual sex theory he calls the prevailing theory of our time. It takes two forms. The first is pre–women's movement, and decidedly male-chauvinist because it "converts sex into an instrument of domination." Women become bunnies, and heterosexuality is replaced "with a not so latent male orientation":

In its magazine formula, it condemns women, flatters the young male, and lavishes on him advice on how to dress, talk, choose his cars and handle his women—all without involvement. The women's movement has shown proper contempt for this view.[3]

The second version of the Casual sex theory seeks an accord with the women's movement by offering "easy access, easy departure, and no long-term ties, but with equal rights for both partners." In his evaluation of both versions of the theory, he has this to say:

> The casual outlook tends to ignore the inevitable complications of most sexual relationships. It lapses into a kind of emotional prudery. . . . The modern casualist is kind of an emotional prude; that is, he tries to deny those emotions that cluster around his sexual life; affection, but not affection alone, loneliness in absence, jealousy, envy, preoccupation, restlessness, anger, hopes for the future. The emotional prude dismisses all these or assumes that sincerity and honesty provide a kind of solvent that breaks down chemically any and all inconvenient and messy feelings. You hope for the future? But I never promised you a future. Why complain? I am emotionally clean, drip-dry. Why not you? This antiseptic view overlooks the element of dirt-farming in sex and marriage. . . . This view overlooks the comic in sex. . . . It overlooks the way sex gets out of control. Sex refuses to stay in the playpen. It tends to defy our advance formulae. It mires each side down in complications that need to be respected. . . . Human sexual life is properly itself only when it is drawn into the self's deeper identity. Thus, against those who reduce sex to the casual, the tradition says sex is important, and should be subjected to discipline like anything important and consequential in human affairs.[4]

However comforting it may be to the womanizer to explain his behavior within the parameters of his sexual-energy theory, the theory has a hollow ring to the listener. By contrast, Dr. May's theory induces the "Ah-ha" or "So that's what it's all about" response. Now the accepting man and the proud man can be seen as members in good standing of the male-chauvinist arm of the Casual sex club, and the philosophers join the ranks of the equal-rights-for-both-sexes arm of the club. The bemoaner, while admitting that he'd like the benefits of membership, recognizes that he can't belong. His sexuality refuses to stay in the playpen. He told me more:

"I had problems with womanizing after a while because I found it very easy to get into relationships, but very difficult to get out of them. I discovered that I'd become emotionally involved. It's hard for me to see how every diehard womanizer isn't a potential homosexual because the gay world offers so many more opportunities for promiscuity, and active womanizers need to discharge their abundant sexual energy without running headlong into the ever-present female walls: marriage and procreation. But I suppose that the male body isn't as intriguing or as beautiful as the female body, so that's one constraint, and then you've got AIDS, the social stigma, and the blatant, ugly, unseemly sexual stuff that goes on in the gay world."

For me, his words offered insight because they provided another slant on the Casual sex theory. It seemed a logical extension of the theory to surmise that homosexual activity might also be included in the womanizer's repertoire. Although the majority of men I interviewed denied any interest or participation in homosexual relationships, a small minority said that they had had some homosexual encounters.

In the good company of Dr. May, I arrived at the conclusion that the womanizer's sexual-energy theory seems to be his rationalized way of avoiding the "dirt-farming" aspects of self-loving and loving of a partner. To quote

Dr. May, I would argue that there is an "emotionally clean" and too easy quality about the idea that men womanize because their sexual energy is stronger than that of other men.

Dr. May's use of the words "emotionally clean," "antiseptic," and "drip-dry" were startling to me for another reason as well. Frequently, I came away from my meetings with womanizers with the feeling that they were impeccable men, too clean to be true; not a hair out of place, no mess or clutter about their persons or their personal spaces. "If appearances could speak," I thought to myself, "then the message is DO NOT DISTURB ME OR RUFFLE MY FEATHERS."

A Personal Flaw

Some womanizers explain their behavior in psychological terms, and attribute it to a character flaw(s). They are willing to acknowledge the behavior as errant, to assume personal responsibility for it, and to seek help either from a psychotherapist or from another resource to assist them in overcoming it. A few of the men I met had succeeded in giving up the womanizing habit. Others were still working on it, and one or two had just begun the process of examining themselves under a psychological microscope.

As will become apparent from the following examples, the sexual-energy theorists and the personal-flaw theorists respond very differently to the question of why they womanize. First, a handsome, socially charming, married man in his mid-forties:

"I don't have much feeling of self-worth. I'm afraid to admit to myself who I am. When I'm pursuing a woman romantically, she thinks I'm exciting and wonderful, but she doesn't know me warts and all, and she doesn't see me on a daily basis to enable her to find the warts."

His wart is his low self-esteem. If he commits himself to one woman, she will discover that he's a nobody, and that's a risk he's not equipped to take. So he plays the field in order to prevent discovery. His wife is one of the women who shouldn't know him. By spreading himself thin through his relationships with other women, he succeeds in warding off intimacy with his wife.

A thirty-nine-year-old bachelor who used to be a womanizer described his flaw as follows:

"I never felt good about myself. I didn't have a sense of completeness, permanence, or self-worth. The incomplete feeling bothered me the most. I was always going out to look for something to complete me. Women were the logical choices. I kept thinking that I'd find the woman who would represent the missing piece. The more I looked, the less I found. I just kept seeing more women all the time."

The image presented here is comparable to the cat chasing his tail. Round and round he goes, all for naught. He stops to rest and then resumes again. The difference between the cat and this man is that the man eventually gave up. Finally, he learned that no woman can make him whole. Later, he became very involved with a religious sect, and gained enough completeness from that association to give up chasing women.

For a fifty-four-year-old rehabilitated womanizer, the recovery process was more complicated. Along the way, he went through a divorce and an ultimately successful bout with alcoholism. He was a womanizer before, during, and long after his marriage. For the explanation of his behavior, he refers to the power of the unconscious mind. He stands out among all the men I talked to as the only one who made this connection directly.

> "I could get back at my mother through womanizing by exploiting women and stringing them along. It felt good. It was a big power trip involving conquest, skill, and imagination. For years, I was unaware of the connection between my womanizing and my feelings about my mother. I went into therapy to overcome the womanizing problem, and that's the first time in my life that I got in touch with my feelings."

This is a man who admits that he used both women and alcohol for the same purpose: to avoid long-standing, unresolved feelings from the past, especially feelings about his mother. It is fair to say, then, that he was addicted to women in the same way that he was addicted to alcohol. Only when he saw it as an illness was he amenable to the treatment.

In contrast to the recovered womanizer is a married man in his late forties who is still going strong. Like the previous three men, he finds a fault within himself that he thinks accounts for his behavior, but he is not tuned in to his unconscious mind. His answer to the "Why do you womanize?" question contains a new twist:

> "I can trace the origins of my womanizing back to high school. Because I was a "gifted" child, I was pushed ahead in school. I was two years younger than my high school classmates. On top of that, I wasn't good-looking or popular. I saw myself as a runt, and this picture of myself remained with me for many years. Womanizing has helped me to overcome that feeling. My wife is not very interested in sex. Her rejection of me makes

me feel unattractive. I need other women to prove that I'm desirable. I love my wife. If she'd be more responsive in bed, I'd stop womanizing."

Here we have a man who feels like a "runt," and unconsciously he chooses for a wife a woman who validates his self-concept. In point of fact, she confirms it by joining into an agreement with him that allows him to philander so long as he prevents sexual diseases from invading their conjugal space. Then, having obtained her permission to do as he pleases, he blames her for causing him to make use of the privilege! No story better illustrates the power of the unconscious. This is a man who is still running from his "runtness" and doesn't know it, so he keeps a wife who doesn't sleep with him very often because, according to his perception, she finds him unattractive, that is, a runt. Therefore, it is her fault that he womanizes to prove that he isn't a runt, and since she's the way she is, his womanizing is really her problem, and if she'd do something about it, everything would be all right! The power lies in the man's unconscious, compulsive replaying of the same old tired script.

All of these stories share a common theme: Something is wrong with me. My personality is missing an important component. I can't repair the gaping hole myself. If I can attract a lot of women, they will make me feel less impaired. In all the stories except the last one, the men acknowledge that womanizing doesn't solve the underlying problem but only camouflages it. The last man acknowledges the problem but blames his wife instead of himself for the continuance of the behavior.

The two examples of men who were recovered womanizers illustrate the importance of admitting the source of the problem and assuming personal responsibility for correcting it as well as the behavior that goes with it. In other words, recovery appears to be a package deal. To accomplish it, you buy the whole package: the underlying problem, the adaptive behavior (womanizing), and the ownership of the responsibility for fixing both. If you buy it piecemeal, you don't obtain the recovery. This is in contrast to alcoholism, which is often successfully treated without attention to its causes, or to certain phobias that are best treated by transferring the responsibility for recovery from the victim to another person or people.

I want to highlight the fact that there are womanizers who do stop womanizing. In succeeding chapters, this will become a significant theme. For now, suffice it to say that I think that those men who attribute their womanizing to a personal flaw are much better candidates for ceasing the behavior than the men who attribute it to the freedom or sexual-energy factors.

Still, we can't lose sight of the fact that the personal flaw or the "gaping hole" can be a very big flaw or a very large hole. If a man thinks that the fault lies within himself for being a womanizer, he is already giant steps ahead of the man who doesn't. Although the first man is more curable than the second, both of them fall under the umbrella of narcissism.

In modern usage, narcissism means excessive self-involvement, but it is frequently misinterpreted to mean self-love. The narcissist, far from loving himself, actually doubts his own worth to such an extent that he needs heavy doses of reassurance.

Every man in this chapter, along with others you will meet later in the book, has been or is a narcissistic type. The narcissist and the addict have much in common. For the addict, steady doses of a toxic substance are required to sustain him. For the narcissist, survival depends on a constant supply of reassurance. Dr. Willard Gaylin, in his book *Rediscovering Love*, explains the similarities between the addict and the narcissist:

The narcissist is concerned with his safety and survival, and like a child he vests his security in others.
Central to that purpose is the need for constant reassurance from all that he is approved and lovable. For
the narcissist popularity and adoration are not luxu-
ries—nor true pleasures; they are insurance policies and
safety measures. Unfortunately, narcissistic reassurance, like narcissistic pleasure, is only a quick fix. Neither truly nourishes. Like a cocaine high or an alcoholic
binge they create an illusion of well-being and safety
that is quickly diminished and more often than not will
lead to a rebound reaction of despair and dread, driving the poor approval addict for yet another and another quick fix.[5]

The freedom-loving womanizer, the sexually driven
womanizer, and the psychologically flawed womanizer
have more similarities than differences. They all con-
duct their relationships with women as if they were riding on a merry-go-round that stops only to pick up new
women as it revolves. Although they differ among themselves about why they ride, they all travel this same or-
bit. Because this is a repetitive behavior, it is tantamount
to an addiction, and because it is circular, it is going
around something rather than through it—as if locked into
a permanent avoidance pattern. What is being avoided?
Surely it must be the commitment to love someone. These
merry-go-round riders are, like children, dizzy, preoccupied with their own needs, and incapable of giving love
to any one woman. Narcissism is the name we can give
to this circular route around love. It might also be called
commitmentphobia except for the fact that many men who
are afraid of commitment to a woman are not womanizers. Womanizing is but one way of avoiding love. Dr.
Gaylin depicts the narcissistic womanizer as follows:

A Don Juan may be seen as a kind of love junky who
never gets the reassurance of real love. He has no idea

what fusion means; he is always separating himself from the very thing he so desperately needs, a loving partner. Women are simply objects to be used as instruments for reassurance. He treats them as mirrors on the wall from whom he is insistently demanding to be told that he is the "loveliest of them all." All he will ever get is a temporary and illusory reassurance, and he will be driven to making the same demand to a thousand different mirrors at a thousand succeeding moments in time. When he asks to be told that he is the most lovable and deserving of everything, he is really asking whether he is worthy of anything at all. Narcissism is a vessel that cannot be filled. If the difference between loving and being loved is the difference between the well and the cistern, the narcissist is a cistern with a leaky bottom or no bottom at all.[6]

In the next chapter we will look more closely at some leaky cisterns. We will want to discover how it all began. Where did things go wrong? How did womanizers become cisterns instead of wells—receivers of reassurance rather than givers of love?

CHAPTER IV

We Never Had the Love That Every Child Oughta Get

"Love is never a one-generational experience," says Dr. George W. Goethals, a well-known psychology professor who conducts a class entitled "Intimacy, Love and Loss." His students are enthralled by the statement and pump him with questions about its meaning.

The professor explains that unhappy relationships between children and parents can lead in later life to profound fears and anxieties about the consequences of love. The greatest fear and the worst consequence centers around the threat of losing the beloved. "If I take the risk to really love someone, and commit myself to him/her, he/she will die or leave me, and then I will be alone and abandoned. That will be too painful for me to tolerate." "Men and women," continues the professor, "bring a difference in liabilities to the table of love."

The most important relationship in early life is between mother and child, but the successful resolution of
the oedipal period for boys means that the mother must
reject her son in favor of his father. The daughter's development does not require this maternal rejection.
Hence, a girl may keep this bond much longer than a
boy and in adulthood she will very likely be less fearful
of commitment and loss of love than her brother. For the
boy, the blow of this rejection by the all-important mother
must be softened by an alliance with, and a psychic in-
corporation of, a good and generous father in whose image he can pattern himself as a future lover. Without
this safety cushion, the boy grows into manhood with
the haunting fear that this terrible rejection will repeat
itself.

What better way to fend off a repeat performance than
to become a womanizer? He escapes all the possibilities
for suffering that might await him if he were to succumb
to the love trap. The wounded man-son concocts a love-
them-a-little-and-leave-them-a-lot potion that works effectively as preventive medicine for the love sickness that
ails him.

As an author and a therapist, I have met many womanizers and heard tales, dispassionately rendered, of
troubled parent-child relationships—tales of death and
desertion, disconnection and disapproval, alcohol and
abuse—and very few tales of love, acceptance, or paternal safety cushions passed from one generation to the
next, and I feel, from time to time, a rush of sympathy
for a group of unloved men who find themselves unable
to love.

Professor Goethals implies that he has been able to
turn his own oedipal rejection to advantage. He recalls
to the class that his beloved mother was a beautiful
blonde, and that he had never been able to date or fall
in love with a blonde despite his best efforts. The initial

rejection by his mother had been too painful to let him take a chance with another blonde. I assume, then, that somewhere along the way he has learned of the existence of redheads and brunettes, and has managed to discover love in another color.

For every woman who now loves or who may yet **love** a womanizer, the task is first to discover from what manner of families these men come and what manner of men they turn out to be, and second to evaluate their potential for learning to love in a brighter color than that which they have inherited from their experiences as children.

The Families of Womanizers

Robin Norwood, in her best-selling book *Women Who Love Too Much*, explains to her readers that no one becomes a woman who loves too much by accident. There is a built-in predisposition resulting from growing up in "dysfunctional" families in which "major aspects of reality are denied and roles remain rigid." [1] Likewise, no man becomes a womanizer by accident. Rather, he becomes one because he is the product of his parents, and something went wrong in the mother-father-son triangulation which didn't get fixed. The following are descriptions of typical faulty triangles extracted from the biographies of womanizers:

1. The mother dies, becomes mentally ill, deserts, or otherwise disengages from the family, and leaves the son in a dyad with the father. In this constellation, the theme is abandonment by the mother, an abandonment more severe than oedipal rejection because the mother's presence is no longer felt. Here, it is important to remember that normally when the oedipal son is rejected by his mother, she does not desert him. She is still physically and emotionally available to nurture and care for him.

2. The mother and son become a dyad to the exclusion of the father. This arrangement has the opposite effect from the previous one. In this model there is an exaggerated attachment to the mother so that the necessary rite of passage to manhood, the oedipal rejection, is delayed, distorted, or initiated by the son instead of the mother, with the probable consequence that the son feels he has triumphed over his father for the affections of his mother. This, in turn, raises the specter of the incest taboo.

3. The mother and father are a disapproving dyad. Here, the questions of abandonment and attachment are blurred. Mother and father seem to behave as a united front. The child feels either rejected or conditionally attached: "We will love you only if you do as we do, and be as we want you to be." The thorny problem is the son's inability to gain parental approval and acceptance for being himself. He is up against a united force more powerful than he can ever be.

4. There is an invisible triangle. Some womanizers described their parents as uninvolved with each other and with their sons. They went through the motions of matrimonial and parental obligation, but kept emotional distance between each other and between themselves and their sons. Often, the sons would turn to grandparents, other relatives, or neighbors for the attachments that were unavailable at home. These families were characterized by extreme underattachment between parents and sons.

Having seen these triangular patterns first in a general way, let us form a more specific focus in order to demonstrate the effects of each pattern on the womanizer/son.

The Son Abandoned by Mother

In this context, abandonment is either a combination of physical and emotional abandonment or exclusively emotional abandonment. It is obvious that if a mother leaves her family, her loss for other family members is both physical and emotional. If she remains in the family, but withdraws significantly from her parenting role, the loss for her son will be an emotional one (though it may also be felt as a withdrawal of physical affection).

One son, Carl, who experienced emotional abandonment before (and after) the age when the oedipal drama unfolds, described it as follows:

"My mother was burned out by the time I came along. She was depressed, had some physical problems, and was having a hard time adjusting to two children, especially on a budget. Eventually, after the birth of my younger brother and sister, she came back to life, but from what I recall and what I've been told, she was out of the picture for my first three years, and was really never affectionate toward me thereafter. She always dealt with me in a backhanded way. She was more like a manager than a mother. She was an enigma to me, someone who was overly concerned with social propriety. My paternal grandmother was a partial substitute for my mother. She played with me, but she died when I was five. My father was more affectionate toward me. He did things with me, taught me valuable skills, but he withdrew from me in my late adolescence when I adopted a life-style that displeased him."

Carl has grown to the age of forty-five as a single man. Although he did enjoy a certain camaraderie with his father, it was not compensation enough for the painful loss of his mother. In his adult life its effects were felt in his relationships with women. "Whenever women push me for more involvement than I can handle, I feel attacked and become scared and symptomatic."

Other men spoke of their mothers' abandonment through death, desertion, or mental illness. Fred's mother died when he was nine.

> "I felt totally abandoned. She was the source of love, warmth, and humor in my family, and when she died she left me with my civilized, unfeeling, and repressive father. He had always been an absentee father anyway. In short order, he sent me off to a strict, Catholic boarding school where words like *sex* and *woman* were never spoken."

The death of a loving mother followed by rejection by his father represents a double abandonment for Fred. From the time of adolescence until his second marriage, he was engaged in a frantic search for women. "There never seemed to be enough women. Even now I think of all the women I may have missed."

Mark was deserted by his mother when he was twelve. He recalls:

> "We never had a good relationship. She was secretive, unexpressive, and very adept at guilt-producing. When she abruptly left my father and me, I thought she was gone for good, but she eventually returned and things got worse. She ridiculed me in front of other people. We fought constantly. All she seemed to care about was getting me out into the work world to earn money. My schoolwork deteriorated badly, and culminated in my dropping out of high school. In my teens, my father and I became drinking buddies. He was an alcoholic and abusive to my mother. He didn't participate in my

upbringing. He was tight-lipped, nonexpressive, and passive."

In this scenario, father and son become buddies, and form an alliance that enables them to stand up to mother. "From then on," said Mark, "I did the macho number in my relationships with women. It was one big power trip."

From infancy to preadolescence, Charles lived with a mentally ill mother and an alcoholic father. There were terrible fights and frequent hospitalizations for his mother. Before his parents divorced, she was permanently hospitalized.

"I have no recollection of my mother, only memories of bad scenes between my parents. After the divorce, my father remarried, and my siblings and I lived with him and our stepmother in various localities. My father died when I was a teenager. Immediately after his death, my stepmother abandoned us to the care of our maternal aunt—a cold woman who cared more for appearances than for us as people. We never saw our stepmother again."

This is a story of abandonment on all fronts: by mother, father, and stepmother. Probably what saved Charles from debilitating mental illness was his good looks, natural athletic ability, and personal charm. These traits earned him the attention and affection of the girls and the admiration of his male peers, and carried him well into adulthood. "I still need the ego boost that I get from being regarded as important and desirable to women. It makes me feel that I'm in control."

The feeling of having been abandoned by mother and/ or her actual departure is a loss that can have devastating consequences in a child's life. The symbiotic connection between child and mother, which begins in the womb and continues in diminishing degrees through infancy and childhood, is the primary source of the child's sense of inner security and well-being. It is a bond of such profound importance that it is comparable to a perilous journey. A misstep here or there, a wrong turn, an unexpected event can leave the traveler alone, standing in the shadow of despair. Likewise, the child embarks on a journey from the safe haven of mother's womb to his eventual independence from her. To accomplish this, he needs her to be there along the way to encourage his attempts at self-reliance, to help him when he falters, and to offer the nurturance, comfort, and discipline that he cannot provide for himself. If the bond is broken in very early childhood, the consequences can be severe, even life-threatening, but if a disruption should occur at any point along the continuum to independence there can be less severe, but long-lasting, repercussions.

Most of us travel into adulthood with at least a suitcase full of repercussions because *perfect* mother-child bondings are relatively rare, but some of us come with a whole trunkload. Everybody knows that it takes less time and effort to unpack a suitcase than a trunk, and anyone who's been to summer camp knows that some people live out of their trunks rather than unpack them.

The men above are people who have been living out of their trunks. Carl's trunk is full of resentment toward women. He sees them as *attackers*. Remember that he described his mother as a woman who abandoned him by withholding affection from him. She is a "manager," a "backhanded" negotiator, an "enigma." To him, women are fear-inspiring, people to run from rather than toward, and he's been on the run from them for most of his adult life. He makes sure that he does the abandoning—always the leaver, never the left.

While Carl appears to have caved in to his conception of the cruel, all-powerful mother, Mark puts up a fight.

He decides to do unto women what women have done unto him. Instead of conceding to the authority of women, as symbolized by the mother who "ridiculed him," "laid guilt trips on him," "forced him to earn money," "never talked to him," and "walked out on him," he would run the "macho number" on women. He would seek out vulnerable, lonely women and play a game of courtship until he had gained the sexual favors he sought, and then he'd be on his way to repeat the process with somebody else. Mark was married for a few years in his twenties but has been a bachelor for over twenty years. Carl has never been married. Their response to abandonment by their punitive mothers has been the "fight" (Mark) and "flight" (Carl) response. Whether you fight mother or run away from her, when all is said and done, the result is the same: In your abandoned, unmarried condition, you stand as a testimonial to mother's power. You're still living out of the trunk she packed for you all those many years ago.

Fred and Charles are also abandoned sons, but their experience of abandonment has a different flavor from Mark's and Carl's. Fred's memories of his mother before she died are positive. She was the source of "love," "warmth," and "humor" in the family. Her death extinguished the family spark and left nine-year-old Fred in the cold presence of an unexpressive father and later in the austere atmosphere of the Catholic boarding school. As soon as he came of age, he went "searching" for women. For him, women were romantic and mysterious creatures who aroused his sexuality and his curiosity. By the age of twenty, he had married "in an attempt to re-create the happy family," but the marriage was short-lived, and before it was over he had begun the search again. In between his first marriage and his second, there were many women. Although he has remained faithful to his second wife, he has "regrets about the women he may have missed." Behind the regrets, I suspect that there is an unconscious fantasy that perhaps somewhere the perfect woman lurks, the woman who will erase the pain of mother's loss and return him to the bliss of that initial bond.

Charles has *no* memories of his mentally ill mother and very few memories of his stepmother. In his late twenties, at a point in his life when he was living alone and feeling lonely, he "fell into" marriage with a woman he had been seeing off and on. "I think I married her for her *maternal* qualities," he told me. "She's the kind of woman who keeps the home in tip-top shape and loves being a mother." He thought that by marrying a "maternal" woman, he might regain the mother he never had, but since he has no picture of his real mother, he keeps looking for the phantom mother—the one who will be capable of filling the emptiness. Nonetheless, throughout their long marriage, Charles has strayed far from the nest with many other women, none of whom were notable for their maternal qualities.

Fred, we might say, has unpacked half his trunk by committing himself to a monogamous relationship, but by his own admission, he has had to use considerable self-restraint to do it. Undoubtedly, the measure of success he has had is attributable to his happy memories of Mom and to his perception of her as the *good, nonpunitive mother*. Charles is still sitting on a full trunk, although as of this writing, he is making serious efforts to unpack it. He is attempting, through therapy, to reopen his personal history book and face the pain of his abandonments rather than continue the habit of trying to control the pain by engaging in stop-and-go relationships with women.

The Son Who Is Too Attached to Mother

The antithesis of the abandoned son is the son who, for one reason or another, is too attached to his mother for too long a period of time. This category of males used to be labeled Mama's boys, and there were pejorative connotations associated with the label. Mama's boys were said to be "sissies" and "wimps." You wouldn't want your daughter to marry one because her entire married life would have to be devoted to winning a contest with his mother over who could take better care of her boy. As long as his mother was alive, healthy, and nearby, went the conventional wisdom, the contest was over before it began because her beloved son would be naturally inclined to prefer bachelorhood to marriage. Better he stick with the woman he knows than gamble with the one he doesn't know!

Today, the Mama's boy tag has gone out of fashion, but it serves my purpose to resurrect it as we examine another kind of family triangle prevalent in the lives of womanizers. Sometimes catastrophic events tip the family scale too far in one direction. The death of a father or his departure from the home due to a divorce can push mother and son into a pseudo-marital relationship. Either the eldest son or the only son becomes the primary candidate to fill the father's shoes, and there are a variety of ways that the mother can behave toward her son to compensate for the loss of her husband.

An eldest son, James, recalled his life with mother after his parent's divorce:

"I was the oldest of four children. At the age of five or six, I became my mother's husband and brother—the responsible one. I was her confidant. She didn't give me any real guidance. Eventually, I took out my aggression on her, and I blamed her for the divorce and the family problems even though I knew that my father had been the cause of many of them. My paternal grandmother lived in the house behind ours. I was her favorite, because I was her first grandchild. She gave me guidance, and she insisted that I get an education. Her death when I was twenty-one was a devastating loss for me. She didn't see me graduate."

Jeff, an only son whose father died when he was five years old, was treated very differently by his mother:

"I was spoiled and overprotected. My mother didn't encourage independence, ambition, or achievement. She emphasized security, like preparing myself to enter the civil service. Although I didn't do that, I could have done better professionally if I hadn't listened to my mother."

In these vignettes we see two different types of Mama's boy. James, the first example, was the boy who became the husband-substitute—the confidant, the responsible child-man. Far from being pampered into "sissyness," he was expected to be the man of the family long before he was ready for the role. To some extent, his grandmother compensated for his mother's inability to meet his childish needs, but not enough to prevent his anger at his mother for placing him in an untenable relationship with her. By making him her confidant, she lured him in too close to her, and by withholding maternal nurturance and guidance, she distanced him at the same time.

As he marched into adulthood, he carried this dual image of women in his trunk. Up to the age of thirty-five, he had few meaningful relationships with women. For the most part, he didn't even date. "I just picked up women for sex," he confessed.

A few years before he married, he decided that it was time to settle down, so he carried on a roller-coaster courtship with a woman, interspersing it with other affairs, drinking bouts, and general irresponsibility. By this time, he had settled down enough in his career to establish himself as the majordomo of a lucrative business. If his relationship with his wife could be called a marriage, it was one in name only. One and a half years after they were wedded, he and his wife separated. He gave her a generous settlement, which he said was motivated out of guilt. "A wife wants to change you, but a mistress takes you the way you are. You can control a mistress, but you can't control a wife. I love the sensual excitement that I get when I first touch a new woman. I'm scared of marriage, but I miss my wife. We tried to reconcile, but I couldn't refrain from infidelity. I tried to keep it a secret, but she found out about it, and that finished the marriage for her." For him, a woman is defined by the dual powers of seduction and deprivation. She giveth (sex) and she taketh away (his identity).

Jeff, the only son who was overprotected and spoiled by his mother, was closer to the prototypical Mama's boy. She tried hard to make a sissy out of him, and in some measure she succeeded. "Don't try to make too much of yourself," she said, "just go for safety and security." Short of refusing to become a civil servant, he did as he was told. He followed a safe, professional route and a safe marital route. He married the lackluster, hometown girl "because that was what you were supposed to do" as soon as you came of marriageable age. He has been married to her for thirty-one years, but has never loved her. Although he's contemplated divorce, he's never had the "courage" to follow through with it.

Behind the scenes, he's been an active womanizer, alternating between one-night stands with call girls and longer-lasting love affairs with women he would have liked to marry. Behaving as if he was still under Mama's thumb, he plays the good boy in public and the bad boy in private. From his mother he acquired the fixed idea that it is wrong to strive for personal happiness. This lesson taught him to settle for less in work and love. "I don't womanize to boost my ego," he says, "I do it because I like to give to women. With the women I care about, I like to give more than I get. I've never been able to be a taker."

Another kind of enmeshed mother-son alliance can result from living with an oppressive husband-father. Although it did not always lead to an exaggerated attachment between mother and son, alcoholism among fathers was prevalent in the lives of the womanizers I met; it afflicted a majority of their fathers, and was the most frequently cited cause of both marital and father-son conflict. In succeeding chapters I will discuss the connection between alcoholism and womanizing in greater detail. Here I am referring to it as one of the causes of an exaggerated mother-son attachment as exemplified by the story below, told by a seasoned womanizer named Steven, now in his sixties:

"I was the oldest son in an Irish family. In my mother's eyes I could do no wrong, even though in her book there was hardly anything you could name that wasn't a sin. My younger brothers resented my special relationship with our mother. Our father was a drinker and a gambler. He was absent during the week due to his work. When he was home, he was strict but not abusive. He gave me much less attention than my mother did."

The boy who could do no wrong has sinned his way through manhood and almost forty years of marriage to an upright woman, leaving a trail of brokenhearted women and fly-by-night lovers. He has done all of this and escaped divorce—the ultimate, unforgivable sin. At his mother's knee and by his father's example, he has been taught, as has many an Irishman, that mothers and wives are the rightful inheritors of virtue. Men, with the possible exception of priests, are ineligible recipients, but they must, as a condition of marriage, erect structures to be displayed as monuments to virtue. So they have long marriages to good women, attend church, go to work, and teach their children moral lessons. While they can *appear* virtuous, they are not genetically equipped, as women are, to *be* virtuous. Thus, there is an unspoken contract between mother and son that says, "I'd like you to be good, but I know that you can't be, so do whatever you need to do as long as you show a good face to the public."

Steven discovered, in short order, that there were many women in the population who weren't nearly as saintly as his mother or wife. In the course of his philandering, he met one or two women who tugged at his heartstrings, women who made him think about divorce, but in the final analysis it was his mother who triumphed. "It would have broken her heart to see me divorced," Steven told me.

There are other reasons aside from a husband's alcoholism that can prod a wife to prefer her son to her husband. Many of the fathers of womanizers were depicted as cold, unfeeling, absent, strict, or abusive, and these character traits are no more endearing to wives than to children. Some mothers were driven by difficult husbands into investing most of their energy in their sons. Don's story was illustrative:

"My father was strict, very old-European in his outlook. He was beloved in the community, but his lovable side was not very evident at home. With me, he was always a disciplinarian. I was more important to my mother than my father was. We were very close. She reserved her support and affection for me but not to the overall detriment of the marriage. Later in my childhood, when my father was sickly, I was my mother's date for social occasions. I was more sensitive to her needs than he was."

If ever there was a pure example of unfinished oedipal business, surely this is it! The rest of Don's story unravels in classic Freudian fashion. He is a well-educated, highly successful professional man. In his twenties, he was married for a few years to a woman he had impregnated. It was a loveless marriage, but, he says, "Since I was a father, I promised my mother I wouldn't leave. As soon as my mother died I left." For most of the past thirty years, he has shown a remarkable penchant for chasing beautiful but impractical female partners. "I always choose women who are noncollegiate types. I can control them better. I see them because they're attractive." He explains his behavior by insisting that he is recapturing his lost youth—all those years when the girls passed him by because he wasn't good-looking. I would explain his behavior by saying that his connection to his mother was too close for comfort.

Again, let me reiterate that the successful resolution of the oedipal complex depends on the mother's rejection of her son in favor of her husband. In Don's case, the reverse has taken place. Mother clearly prefers her son, and in so doing she brings him to the brink of violating the incest taboo. Since mother is the one girl he's not supposed to have, it is more than coincidental that her son has kept himself so busy with girls he's not supposed to have.

These Mama's boys' exaggerated attachments to their

mothers have had far-reaching effects on their adult love lives. Their stories tend to substantiate the old, conventional wisdom that Mama's boys are bad bets for marriage partners. Whether they marry or not seems to be irrelevant. Collectively, they share the most damnable quality—an unflinching loyalty to Mama. The loyalty, in turn, creates other qualities—either an uncanny ability to lead a double life or a total inability to connect with another woman. In order to keep their vows to mother, the married men make things look good on the surface by maintaining lifeless marriages, but behind the marital window dressing, they lead turbid love lives. The unmarried remain faithful to their mothers by refusing to replace them. Be they husbands or bachelors, their hearts belong to Mama.

The Son of Disapproving Parents

In contrast to the Mama's boys are the boys who belong to neither Mama nor Papa. They don't quite measure up to their parents' standards. Although in early childhood they may have enjoyed a good relationship with one or both of their parents, when they reach school age the relationship begins to deteriorate. It can come as a shock to a child to fall so precipitously out of his parents' favor, especially since he is unaccustomed to the notion that parental love can come with strings attached. The awareness that holding a place in their affections is a reward to be earned rather than a gift to be given will be interpreted by the child as a rejection and a threat to his security. Unconsciously, he says to himself, "I'm not the person they want me to be; therefore I'm unlovable and a failure," and, "If I can't count on Mom and Dad to love and support me, I can't count on anybody."

Jack's struggle with his parents is instructive:

"I thought I had a good relationship with my mother. She was a very strong woman with a sharp mind. She was always in control, and evidenced no weaknesses. She was a superstar—respected, popular, good-looking. She expected me to set an example for my two younger brothers. My father was a community leader. He, too, had no visible weaknesses. He was fearless, extremely successful, good-looking, and a superstar. My parents were the perfect type. They had a following. Everybody emulated them. I could never approach their standard. I wasn't on their level. They were always telling me that I could do better. I never got approval. That was the big deprivation in my childhood. Otherwise, I was raised with a silver spoon."

Jack was sent off to boarding school during his high school years. When he hit college, he went on a binge "with a vengeance." He drank, took drugs, and womanized his way through college, studying just enough to get by. Finally, toward the end of his senior year, this life-style got the better of him. He gave up the alcohol and the drugs and turned to religion for strength. He did not, however, give up womanizing. With the exception of one or two long-term relationships, his romantic life has consisted of brief liaisons with several women simultaneously.

At first, he was just pleased to discover that he was appealing to so many women, and that he didn't need the back-up of alcohol or drugs to receive their attention. Later, he became hooked on the approval that women gave him, and as time passed he found that he needed heavy doses of it to sustain him. Until very recently, he never entertained the thought of commitment or marriage, but gradually he has been able to break his "approval" habit by recognizing that he would have to be a best friend to himself. All the years of parental criticism had groomed him into becoming his own worst critic. "I wanted to like myself so much, but I've had to work hard to make it happen."

Sam learned in early adolescence that he would have to rely on himself, that he couldn't count on his parents for much of anything:

> "Almost as soon as I could talk, I didn't get along with my mother. Among her five children I was the most assertive, and once that became apparent we were at loggerheads over who was in charge. She would have been happier without children. She was a high achiever who should have had a career. Now, I think of her as someone who was terrified of men. My father liked me a lot when I was young, because I excelled in school, but he was absent much of the time. As I got older he was increasingly withdrawn from the family. By the time I reached adolescence, my willful behavior put me on a collision course with my father. I was not respectful of authority. My behavior was wild. Finally, my father kicked me out of the house. He built a separate dwelling on the property which served as my home until I went to college. From the age of fourteen through my college years, I supported myself by playing poker. My parents refused to give me money."

Sam's history reads very much like Jack's without the religious conversion. His binge with alcohol and drugs started earlier and lasted longer. The seeds of his womanizing behavior were sown in high school when he began a pattern of starting a relationship, feeling comfortable in it, and then moving along to another girl. Throughout college and graduate school, his life was a "sexual free-for-all" with liberal supplements of alcohol and drugs.

At the age of twenty-seven, he met the love of his life, but he kept on philandering for the three years of their courtship until the death of his best friend turned a marriage proposal from his girlfriend into an offer he couldn't refuse. For the first six years of the marriage, he was 100 percent faithful. As the marriage progressed, both husband and wife became "serious careerists" and gradually pulled away from each other. Toward the end, he had a telepathic feeling that she was having an affair. Without further ado, he kicked her out of the house. "I had terrible pain," he says, "which I handled by working hard, screwing around, and playing squash." After six months the pain had subsided, but the memory of being hurt stayed with him. Losing the marriage felt to him like the loss of paradise. The married years were the best years of his life, a time of privacy and a time to relinquish the wildness of his youth. After the breakup, he was afraid to fall in love again. With the exception of one short relationship, he has returned to womanizing.

Jack's and Sam's promiscuous behavior reflects the parental disapproval that each of them received. By behaving disreputably, they validated their parents' perceptions of them as undeserving sons. Then, in order to prevent self-destruction, they sought redemption. They became *converts*—Jack a religious convert and Sam a marital convert. The problem with conversions, though, is that they are halfway measures. They rarely finish the business. Jack's conversion released him from alcohol, drugs, womanizing, and self-hatred, but it hasn't yet brought him the love that he wants. Sam's conversion released him permanently from toxic addiction, but only temporarily from addiction to women.

Converts rely heavily on *external* rather than *internal* resources to overcome life's hurdles. Thus they leave themselves open to the temptation of searching for more and better props from the outside world instead of looking inside themselves for the ingredients and the evidence of lovability. In the final analysis, self-love begets the love of others. The original deprivation of parental approval, at a time in life when it is crucial to one's self-esteem, helps explain why conversion is so appealing. The convert attempts, through religion, marriage, or some other bulwark, to obtain the emotional reinforcement that his parents didn't provide for him.

All in all, a conversion (unless it is extreme, as membership in a cult would be) is not a bad way for a deprived adult to begin the process of regrowth. It can represent a kind of "flight into health," but it carries with it the necessity to recognize when the time has come to move away from reliance on the prop toward reliance on oneself.

Jack's story has optimistic signs, because he has arrived at that crossroads and appears to have selected the self-reliant path—in his words, "be becoming my own best friend." Sam has not recovered enough from the failure of his conversion to turn himself over to himself.

The Unattached Son

When I started talking with womanizers, I was introduced to Moms and Dads who, while not necessarily *bad* parents—though some were blatantly so—were unresourceful, uninterested, and/or overwhelmed by their roles. At first I assumed that these characteristics explained the sons' feelings of detachment from them, but as I listened further, an unmistakable similarity among all the sons in this category shed more light on the matter: They all appeared to be more precocious than their

parents, so that at relatively early ages they had sur-
passed them in intelligence, achievement, and general
capability. This discovery led me to regard the detachment between the sons and their parents as resulting more
from *mutual incompatibility* than from one-sided parental inadequacy.

In Chapter III, I gave an illustration of a man who fits
this category—the man who thought of himself as a runt.
His name is Phillip. Here he is again:

> "My mother lacked patience. Having three kids pushed
> her too hard, and having one who was exceptionally
> bright pushed her even harder. She was only involved
> in my life to the degree that she was capable, and she
> wasn't very capable. She could do the domestic stuff,
> but any nurturing I got came from my grandmothers.
> My father was an alcoholic, and an abusive one at that.
> By the age of seven, I had totally overwhelmed both
> my parents. Any authority that they tried to exercise, I
> defied. When I was eight, I wrote a novel which they
> burned because it wasn't a homework assignment. I
> had an unhappy childhood. For the most part, I was
> left alone. My only happy times were with my grand-
> parents."

This chapter of Phillip's autobiography suggests that
he was a child who was responsible for his own upbringing. Neither of his parents was equipped to rear him. He
received very little affection, no guidance, and a steady
diet of paternal abuse. His parents were no match for
him intellectually.

There were echoes of a similar disparity in Ben's
background:

> "My parents were intent on my receiving an educa-
> tion, but I went further than they ever thought I could.
> In a way, I went so far that they lost me altogether. As

a child, I felt that I was burden to them so I never had a desire to procreate. My mother was more a guardian than a mother. She was nice enough, but she couldn't teach me much. There was a lot of emphasis on right and wrong. My father was a solid person, more objective, fun-loving, and attentive than my mother was, but he was not well-educated (nor was mother). After high school, when I went on to college and then to a prestigious graduate school, where I later taught, I became the apple of my parents' eye."

These parents were much better-disposed than the previous set, but clearly there was a distance between them and their son—an unbridgeable gap. One can hypothesize that Ben, at some point in his childhood, had already gone beyond his parents. Because of their intellectual limitations, they were restricted in their ability to help him grow.

Again in the following two sketches we hear the same theme with some significant variations:

Tom: "My mother was very old-school. You couldn't talk to her. I was one of seven children. We were treated like a group, not like individual personalities. My mother saw to it that we were clothed and fed, and she sacrificed for us. My father was a drinker, a passive person who couldn't control his children. He used the belt when we got out of hand. He was too busy to give us much time. Outside the home, he was a very friendly guy who everybody knew and liked. When I was an adult, I learned that he had been a womanizer. We received very little guidance from either parent. We were on our own."

Marty: "My mother was a typical Italian Mom. She wanted me to eat, work (for money), and have my friends over. She yelled a lot, but she could be affectionate too. She didn't understand me or my life-style preferences. I rebelled against the work-ethic standard. My father was very smart, a professional man, but a heavy-handed father. He had a terrible temper, and would kick the shit out of you when he felt like it. His thinking was strict and rigid. He told me that he had made two mistakes in life: getting married and having kids. He was a womanizer. From him, I got the idea that marriage was a sacrifice, a choice to be avoided."

Both of these sons are college-educated men. Tom has a professional career, and Marty divides his time between rock music and human services. Neither of them had parents who could be helpful to them in any context other than meeting basic needs for food, clothing, and shelter. Their accomplishments are the result of their own efforts. In each case, there were abusive fathers.

For these men, womanizing has become a way of life. They've grown up accustomed to detachment. Without strong connections to either parent, they stepped prematurely into self-reliance. They learned to connect with themselves, but not with other people. Unlike the sons with disapproving parents who were forced into interaction with their parents, these boys had to make do on their own. In talking with them, I had the sense that they didn't understand the value of connectedness in human life. Never having felt connected, they didn't seem to know what they were missing.

Among the men in Chapter III who attributed their womanizing to the sexual-energy factor, the majority were *unattached sons*—men who were looking for women from whom they could receive sexual gratification. Although two of the men above were married, one for many years, they were no more attached to their wives than their parents had been to them. Women came and went in their lives with clocklike regularity. Once in a while, one or another woman would arouse fond feelings in such a man, but he would assume from the start of the affair to its conclusion that these feelings are fleeting—troublesome perhaps, but in the long run insignificant. *"C'est la vie,"* he says too easily.

In Summary

The families of womanizers were characterized by four triangular patterns, each of which affects the son in a distinct way. The diagrams below illustrate the patterns. Dotted lines represent *disconnections*. Dark lines represent *strong* connections. Dashes represent *weak* connections.

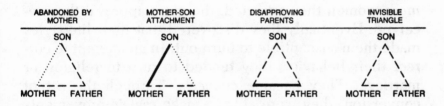

ABANDONED BY MOTHER	MOTHER-SON ATTACHMENT	DISAPPROVING PARENTS	INVISIBLE TRIANGLE
SON	SON	SON	SON
MOTHER FATHER	MOTHER FATHER	MOTHER FATHER	MOTHER FATHER

In their behavior with women, the adult sons *abandoned by their mothers* were still playing out a script with them. Either they used women to maintain the *fight* with their mothers, or they used them to *flee* their mothers by loving and *leaving* as many women as they could. Some abandoned sons, however, were able with effort, insight, and determination to distance themselves enough from the script with their mothers to reduce or cease their womanizing behavior.

The womanizer sons who were too *attached to their*

mothers became the kinds of men who, if married, remained in long-standing, dull marriages—a reflection of stubborn loyalty rather than genuine love. Behind the scenes, they carried on countless affairs with women. The loyalty was derived from their overinvolved relationships with their mothers, to whom they still had an allegiance. It was as if they were saying, "Don't worry, Mom, we won't let you down. We'll look as good as you want us to look, because that is what you expect from us in return for all that you gave us." The unmarried sons took it a step further by showing their mothers that they were irreplaceable. They had many women, but not one of the lot could ever fill Mama's big shoes.

Disapproved sons behaved disreputably in adult life. They combined womanizing with excessive alcohol and drug use, and with generalized irresponsibility. They became "approval junkies," and used women to shore up their terrible self-images. With their insatiable need for approval, they were compelled to find as many women as possible to prove that they had personal appeal. The more women they attracted, the more approval they received. Eventually they discovered that their life-styles made them susceptible to burn-out. In an attempt to correct their behavior, they tended to turn to religion or marriage. They became *converts*. Through the act of conversion, they were able to make real improvements in their behavior, but not necessarily to reach the goals that they had set for themselves. True self-reliance was difficult for them to attain.

Finally, we met the *unattached sons*, the men who had turned womanizing into a way of life. Whether married or single, they were distinguished by their inability to form meaningful connections to women or to understand what it felt like to be bonded with another human being. As children, they were left to themselves so much that they became prematurely self-reliant. They learned how to connect with themselves, but not with other people.

"Love is not a one-generational experience," as the professor told the class. The men in these pages seem, for the most part, to be people who never had the opportunity to grow up. Their childhoods were unhappy, and they carried that pain in their adult trunks (usually without knowing that they had it) and were crippled by the weight. At every stop, they pulled out pieces of their pasts and reenacted them with women—as if they were passengers on a train that gave the illusion of forward motion while in reality never left the station. Nonetheless, as sad and hopeless as their stories seemed to be, here and there an optimistic note was struck. Some men did move forward.

PART II

The Dance
That They Do

Chapter V

The Dancers and
the Dance

    If a man asks you to dance with him, and you accept his invitation, you become partners for the duration of the dance. Likewise, if a womanizer asks you to consort with him, and you accept his offer, you become his partner in the *activity of womanizing*. While you will definitely not be his only partner, you will be *one* of them, and you will have earned your position by agreeing to participate. Once you become a participant, you are as accountable as he is for whatever happens between the two of you, but when the lightning strikes and the pain begins, you will find it very difficult to acknowledge your own complicity. You will be hurt and angry, and your natural tendency will be to seek relief through blame or retaliation, but eventually you will discover that these methods compound the pain instead of relieving it.

If he feels some remorse for having hurt you, it will be an insufficient motive for restoring the partnership to its former glory, and if he feels no remorse, you are left alone with your bag of blames and retaliatory fantasies. Undoubtedly you will find yourself screaming or crying on more solitary evenings than you will ever want to admit or remember, but you will reach catharsis only when you have arrived at your own reckoning place and can confess the truth to yourself: "I got myself into this. He didn't get me into it." Then you, like the woman you met in our first two chapters, will have to begin the rehabilitation process.

So far you have learned that men and women are predisposed to engage in this peculiar dance of love known as womanizing through accidents of birth, by being born into families with certain psychopathological characteristics. These in turn influence the character development of the children who later become womanizers or women who are womanized. Before I can tell you what to do about the womanizer in your life or how to design your own rehabilitation program, I want to make sure that you know a little more about yourself and a little more about him, and I want to describe for you the kind of dances I think you do together.

In thinking about womanizing, the dance analogy comes naturally. Womanizing seems to me to be a *choreographed* activity. The steps, the moves, the dips, the turns, the twists, and even the improvisational pieces of the dance, are prearranged. After a while, many womanizers and their female partners say *the same things* about how they behave with their partners. They know what they're going to do *before* they do it, and the challenge lies in doing it *better* each time around the floor. Just as there are partners who are better at waltzing than they are at jitterbugging, there are certain types of women who are more natural partners to certain types of womanizers.

What I am about to do is to pair up the best-suited partners and then let you watch them on the dance floor. If you find yourself among the dancers, let that be a signal to you to begin creating another dance.

The Bimbo and the Conqueror—Waltz Me Around Again, Willy

There are many examples of prominent men who might be classified as Conquerors. Often, they are powerful, well-known, middle-aged public figures who squire young, beautiful women who earn the Bimbo label because they are so much younger and less accomplished than the Conquerors who pursue them. At first blush, the Bimbo and the Conqueror appear to be improbable partners. In prestige, age, background, social position, they seem to be the antithesis of one another.

For the compulsive womanizer who is the Conqueror type, it is essential that there be a glaring disparity (or disparities) between him and his female partner. He has to be the top dog in the relationship—the *lead dancer.* His ideal partner is the woman who knows her place. She is always the *follower*, never the improviser.

Don, a Conqueror: "I like to be seen with pretty women. I always choose women who are beneath me socially. I can control them better."

While I dislike the term *bimbo* for its potential to disparage women in general, I am using it here, in the absence of a better one, for the sole purpose of describing a type of woman who is a natural companion for the Conqueror. She is the kind of woman who lets herself be led. The Conqueror and the Bimbo are co-dependent partners. The columns below illustrate the way that they complement each other:

The Bimbo	The Conqueror
Her family	*His family*
Daddy's girl—passive mother	Mama's boy—weak or absent father
Disapproving parents	Disapproving parents
Her profile	*His profile*
She doesn't make overt demands on him. She's compliant, will do whatever he wants.	He has to be in control. He calls the shots.
She's young and/or beautiful.	He is older and successful.
She's often a nonprofessional, not well off financially, a gold digger.	He is apt to be professional with a high income.
She's afraid of the adult responsibility that goes with intimacy and marriage. She wants only to be taken care of.	He's either a married man or a confirmed bachelor and runs from intimacy.
She's sexy and generous with her sexuality.	He's a sexual dynamo.
She doesn't try too hard to triumph over his other women. She will overlook rather than protest his womanizing, if she thinks that her objections will force him to leave her.	His need for conquest means that he always has or is seeking another woman or women.

Her profile	*His profile*
She wants caretaking and leadership. She's dependent and feels helpless without a caretaking male.	He wants his sexual needs met. He likes his freedom, and feels entitled to it. He is often a drinker or a drug user who needs these stimulants to make him appear independent and in charge.
She lets him go.	He moves on.

Having placed this perfectly matched couple on the dance floor, I'd like you to watch them perform. Notice how easily she takes her cues from him, how effortless it is for her to follow his lead.

WALTZING AROUND WITH WILLY THE CONQUEROR

The Conqueror is a "ballsy" guy. There's an air of authority about him. Not necessarily handsome and certainly not warm and fuzzy, he nonetheless has a penchant for knowing what to do, what to say, what he likes and whom he likes. He is a "can-do" person, a born administrator, a man's kind of man. Put him at the helm and the boat will go where he wants it to go. He likes to tackle tough assignments, and he likes to come out on the winning end of every challenge.

> **Don:** "I like the challenge of conquering a new woman. It's the same way a hunter feels when he corners his prey."

Each fresh victory gives him an adrenaline high and readies him for the next conquest. The Conqueror selects challenges that come with a prestigious label. He is disciplined in pursuit of *wealth, power, and influence.*

More often than not, he is the *boss* of his business or professional concern, and he has arrived there through single-minded diligence and a strong desire to control. (Many of the Conquerors I met told me that they had to be their own bosses. The idea of accountability to a superior was repugnant to them.)

In order to complete or put the finishing touch on his success package, *he needs to be seen in the company of young, beautiful, unassertive women.* They are his visible proof of prowess, worthiness, masculinity, and success, and their attraction to him has an additional psychological benefit. "If I can get the most desirable women to fall for me, I must be special," he tells himself. Hal is an example:

> "I have to be in control with women. I am aggressive sexually. I might date one person longer than another, but I'd be totally unfaithful. Everyone I see is young and pretty. That's why I see them. For them I'm a father figure. They help me maintain my youthfulness."

One woman's approval is never enough, however. He requires multiple doses of feminine attention.

He spots her easily on the dance floor. She has the right physical attributes. Like most pretty girls, she is *waiting* to be approached. She is accustomed to having men move toward her. No need for her to make an overture in their direction. Still, she looks tentative and a little helpless just standing there. The surefooted Conqueror comes to her rescue, and he senses gratitude and relief in every muscle of her body as he leads her into the dance. She is demure, attentive to his words and gestures, genuinely in awe of his ability to take charge, and subliminally aware of his success. This is *the* man she's been waiting for, the caretaker she has to have, the strong man she knows she deserves.

Gloria: "I just waited for someone to take me in. I did everything he asked me to and didn't ask for much from him. He controlled me completely. I overlooked his affairs. I was dependent and wanted a Daddy. There's a chemistry between me and a man like this. He only wanted me to look pretty. He didn't want to see me involved in household drudgery or bickering like a wife would."

So what if her Conqueror is graying a bit around the edges; he will be as competent at leading her through the jungle of life as he is at steering her around a crowded ballroom. He knows he's almost got her, but the proof of the pudding, the conquest itself, awaits in the bedroom. If she resists initially, he's patient, but with the right moves and time on his side, he triumphs. In the event that her Conqueror happens to be a married man, she may have the luxury of his steady but part-time company for a long period of time, and while she will yearn for full-time status, she will very likely settle for what she gets. If he is a single man, the chances are better than average that he will terminate the relationship with the conquest. Sometimes, if the time is just right, and he thinks he should be married, he might lead her to the altar, but after the honeymoon is over, he will return to waltzing around the dance floor with as many lovely Susies and Sallys as he can find. *Or* he will wander off in search of somebody special to keep on the side until the inevitable time when he tires of her, his wife, or both of them.

Some Bimbos are so accustomed to their role that they become invulnerable to being hurt by Conquerors. Like their male counterparts, they learn through experience that there are other Conquerors around the corner just as there are other Bimbos. For the novice, however, abandonment by the Conqueror can be a devastating experience. It takes her many years and many spins around the dance floor before she learns to lower her expectations of a man to the nadir that the seasoned Bimbo reaches. If she's lucky, she breaks the pattern after the first or second bruising, and learns to control her dependency and become more self-reliant. Then, and only then, can she resist seduction by the Conqueror.

The Conqueror usually exhibits amazing staying power. In his gallery of relationships, he rarely presents himself as a victim. He seems impervious to hurt, except perhaps by a failed marriage, and then it appears to be the failure rather than the loss of the spouse that has wounded him. Unlike other types of womanizers, he registers little if any guilt about his behavior and the heartbreak it may have caused. He can carry on with women for many years, never seeming to tire of the practice, and able to maintain a sexual schedule that would lead most mortal men to an early death. In my conversations with Conquerors over fifty, I did hear rumblings about the attractiveness of commitments and subtle hints that so much sexual activity does take its toll, but there was a reluctance in the admission. Most said that they had less energy for the hunt than they used to have, but if the right opportunity were to present itself—well, yes, that would be tempting.

The Princess and the Charmer—the Light Fantastic

The Princess and the Charmer make a stunning pair not only because they are good-looking, but also because they are apt to be smart, savvy, smooth, well-educated, funny, and fun. More often than not, they are attractive, accom-

plished, successful professionals. They're incurably romantic. Between them, there is a similarity and an
equality that sets them apart from the Bimbo and the
Conqueror.

At the dance, the Charmer is more subtle than the
Conqueror. In his every word and gesture, he presents
himself as a man who loves and adores women. He lacks
the Conqueror's bravado, and is more discriminating in
his selection of a partner. He looks for signs of classi-
ness—the way she wears her hair, the quality of her
clothes, the way she moves and speaks, her distinctive-
ness. When he approaches her, his eyes speak first, then
come the gentle touch, the modest blush, the hints of
flattery, respect, and care for her, the fleeting glance, the
dash of humor that puts them both at ease, and finally
the effortless execution of the dance.

> **Bruce, a bonafide Charmer:** "I am romantic and gentle.
> I woo with flowers, champagne, passion, and affection.
> Because I often don't feel very much for the person,
> and don't even know what I'm feeling about anything
> a good deal of the time, I have to *act* like I'm feeling.
> I'm actually a closed sort of person. I like women who
> are intelligent, attractive, sexual, and sensuous—women
> who like to travel to exotic places."

It's as if the Charmer and the Princess know, without
benefit of words, that they are kindred spirits, that they
are made for one another, that they are destined to dance
together. The Charmer has no equal in his ability to con-
vey chemistry, and he has a sixth sense for sniffing out
those Princesses who are ready to receive it. The Princess, in fact, thrives on it. She cannot conceive of enter-
ing into any relationship where the chemistry isn't
apparent from the outset. Consummate romantic that she
is, she has tunnel vision when it comes to love. For her,
love is defined by the omnipresence of an internal volcano—a volcano that she hopes will be eternal. Because

her hopes are high and because the Charmer is the most insidious of womanizers, the Princess is extremely susceptible to heartbreak. She is truly in love with the Charmer, but his eyes are not only for her.

Meanwhile, before his eyes wander again, the Princess and the Charmer dance gracefully around the floor. Here's how they look:

The Princess	The Charmer
Her family	*His family*
Distant father/depressed mother	Abandoned son
Loss of a parent(s)	Invisible triangle
Her profile	*His profile*
She is talented, educated, attractive, successful.	He is smart, educated, attractive, successful.
She is dependent, but looks independent.	He feels empty inside, but looks content and happy on the outside.
She is warm, outgoing, socially polished.	He is warm, outgoing, socially polished.
She is passionate. Falls madly in love.	He is passionate. He makes love madly.
She yearns for love and loves to yearn.	He is elusive. He hides his warts.
She shows her vulnerability.	He is reassuring.
She likes to probe his inner depths.	He is secretive and mysterious.
She tries and tries to understand him, and blames herself for having failed in the relationship.	He vanishes before she gets to know him.
She mourns.	He finds another Princess.

Before we watch the dance from its inception to its cruel conclusion, one explanation of a point on the above profile is in order. The Princess is a woman whose *long-ing* for love far exceeds her desire to actually have it. This is undoubtedly related to the distant relationship she had with her father—the mysterious first love of her life. Having grown accustomed to longing for her father, she feels more secure in the longing state than in the loving state. In their book *Smart Women, Foolish Choices,* authors Kinder and Cowan describe this phenomenon in women:

> Love and longing are confused and mistakenly linked. Longing or unrequited love is an extremely powerful feeling. . . . Girls not blessed with affectionate fathers may develop intense feelings of longing for the father's contact and love. As these girls become more verbal and can label their experiences and feelings, they come to believe that "longing" and "love" are one. In essence, an identity is established between "wanting" and the concept of love. . . . Women who confuse longing with love find it difficult to feel "in love" if their feelings toward a man are reciprocated. They associate love not with "having" but with "wanting."[1]

THE LIGHT FANTASTIC

The Charmer is graceful and smooth. He glides through his romantic relationships with style and agility, and he has an uncanny ability to make a woman feel special. She thinks she has hooked the best "catch" in the masculine sea because he is so gifted at image-making. Here is Bruce again:

> "I like having affairs because I don't have to see someone on a daily basis. This permits me to hide my flaws. It conceals my low self-esteem. I know that women will respond to me because I appear flirtatious, charming, confident, and flattering."

Once the Princess attaches her romantic hopes to her illusion of the Charmer's perfection, she is on the road to heartbreak. Before the journey ends, however, the Charmer will have beguiled his Princess at every turn in the dance.

Bruce: "In order to extricate myself from affairs, I begin slowly to find faults with my partner, and gradually I increase the intensity of my criticisms, accompanying them with announcements about my busy schedule and my unavailability."

The Princess is dazzled by her partner. He sweeps her off her feet into the fictional land of romance where messages from the brain are drowned out by loud beats from the heart. She wants to believe her own romantic fairy tale. As Julie puts it:

"When he shines his light on you, you feel instantaneous self-worth, the kind of self-esteem you can't give to yourself. It feels like a miracle has happened. Then you tell yourself with very little effort, 'This guy is so charming. I must be very special to have landed him.' Now I never have to worry again about being alone. Life seems to be an endless party. He's so charming; we're so charming together that everybody comments on what a wonderful pair we are."

The Princess deplores the nitty-gritty routines of normal heterosexual relationships. They're for ordinary folks, but not for her. She doesn't want to stoop to awkward scenarios in which men and women struggle over messy little domestic or interpersonal matters and make fools of themselves for their own or the neighbors' benefit. The Princess is convinced that she's above all that. She is overqualified for *relationship drudgery*. From her perspective, she is a talented scavenger of the soul, a man's ideal intimate partner. When she discovers that intimacy is the very condition the Charmer *least* desires, she falls so far and so fast from her own pedestal that personal injury is assured. Ben, an experienced Charmer, reveals how he avoids intimacy and induces female injury:

"In high school I began to recognize that I had charm. The jocks would be mad at me because I could talk easily to girls. By the time I hit college I was playing a big field. With women I'm a gentleman. I'm charming with mannerisms, words, and focus, but I've never been interested in marriage. I feel guilty about the women I've hurt, but it's never been intentional. I have said 'I love you' a few times, but the game is really sexual. I lose interest eventually. The turnoff could be something as simple as a grammar slip. If the sex is great, though, the relationship might last longer."

Very frequently, the Princess opts for successive rounds of injury instead of one successful round of intimacy.

The major distinction between the Bimbo and the Princess is that the Bimbo looks and acts dependent while the Princess looks independent but acts dependent. Thus, the Princess is a more complex character than the Bimbo is, and because she chooses for a partner the most mysterious and subtle womanizer of the lot, she has a harder time unraveling the emotional labyrinth that has ensnared her. Her romantic nature compounds her dilemma. She submits to her illusional conception of romance with as much fervor as she submits to the Charmer. Recovery for her is a two-part process which requires that she: 1) give up the lover (not necessarily because she chooses to, but because he usually rejects her or refuses to commit herself to her); 2) give up her romance with romance! As hard as the first step is, the second step can be harder still. Julie explains:

"It takes a long time to acknowledge the first shock waves even though they may have been there much earlier, but inevitably you discover that he has moved on to other women. You say, 'What do I do now?' You spend more and more time alone until finally you have to let him go, but you resist right down to the last gasp."

The Adventuress and the Adventurer—Dirty Dancing

Although Pablo Picasso throughout his long life was the consummate womanizer—the Conqueror, the Charmer, the Adventurer, and the universal narcissist rolled into one—in his relationship with Marie-Thérèse Walter, he was a classic example of the *Adventurer* and she was the embodiment of the *Adventuress*. He was a middle-aged married man when he met her, and she was a beautiful teenager whom he spotted in a crowd exiting a Paris Metro station. His most recent biographer, Arianna Stassinopoulos Huffington, describes the introduction of the two lovers: "I'm Picasso! You and I will do great things together." Marie-Thérèse represented his most sexually passionate experience. The initial stages of their courtship throbbed with passion and adventure. In the company of his wife and his three-year-old son, Picasso went on a summer vacation near a children's camp that Marie-Thérèse was attending, and there, in absolute secrecy, they began their affair. Huffington says further:

> It was an ingenious arrangement that delighted Picasso not only because of its watertight secrecy but also because of its perversity. The idea of visiting his young mistress at a children's camp added a frisson of risk, surrealism and masquerade to a relationship that was already bristling with sexual passion, a passion that

continued to thrive on the often violent subjugation of the "woman-child" to her lover's will. . . . The fact that Marie-Thérèse was legally under age and in a children's camp was a mainspring of Picasso's sexual ardor. At that time in France the corruption of a minor could result in a severe prison sentence, but flouting the law was part of the excitement that fired his passion.[2]

For the Adventuress and the Adventurer, love is a high-risk game. If each of them is a married person, or if only one of them is, they are the kind of pair who put their lives on the line for the surreptitious moments they share together. They're emotional gamblers who frequently ante up with other people's feelings as well as their own. The thrill in their match is the thrill of deceit. They need to "cheat on" someone. Like teenagers experimenting with alcohol, they get as much of their fun from the challenge of not being caught as they get from the activity itself. Brad was a full-fledged Adventurer. Listen to his tale of deceit:

"I was good at cheating people. I cheated with women and I cheated on the job."

Should they happen to be an unmarried pair, their attachment often has a rebellious flavor. She chooses him because she knows that her parents would hate him for his inferior social status or his disreputable life-style, but these are the characteristics that attract her to him. Give her the choice between a humdrum bourgeois existence and unpredictable adventurousness, and she will sacrifice the tedium she knows for the razzle-dazzle she doesn't know.

Catherine remembers: "Nothing bothered him. He'd do anything on a whim. He'd travel and go places. He liked to drag race."

Laura, recalling life with her husband: "He had to have sex all the time. He liked to have fun. He was a big spender. Sometimes he'd drink and drive at the same time. He slept with so many women that I was constantly afraid that I'd wake up one morning and learn that I had AIDS."

He chooses her because she seems bored with her life, and he can feel a flame of suppressed adventurousness waiting to be ignited, or because he responds to the unfailing magnetic pull that draws two rebels together.

The Adventurer is a born rebel on a perpetual search for rebellious female partners. Among womanizers, he is the most *juvenile*. Adolescence is never over for him, and since there are so many pretty, feminine rebels in his midst, he likes to sample all the varieties rather than settle in with one. The Adventurer, like most adolescents, is an *experimenter*. He believes that experience is the best teacher, and that the more women he experiences the more he will learn about them. Usually he turns out to be correct. He does become knowledgeable about women, but he uses the knowledge to manipulate them. His spirit of adventurous experimentation is not limited for its expression to relationships with women, however. Drugs, alcohol, kinky sex, and/or daring athletic or vehicular adventures excite him too. As he ages, the Adventurer may relinquish some of the more reckless, life-threatening components of his life-style, but he reasons that womanizing is safer stuff (even in the face of AIDS) as long as he is relatively cautious in his selection of sexual partners. If he gives up womanizing at all, the odds are that it will be the *last* erasure on his bad-habit list.

The Adventuress presents herself in two distinct guises. One kind of Adventuress looks bored, somewhat restless, and rather obvious in the way she demonstrates that she is hankering for a stimulating experience. The other kind has a visible gleam in her eye and the right amount of flirtatious assertiveness to go with it. Both kinds are attractive in appearance and representative of a wider age and socioeconomic range than the Bimbos or the Princesses. Neither of the two Adventuresses are shy, nor do they care whether they are the "approachees" or the "approachers" with men. For them, the goal is heterosexual adventure, and the means of reaching their destination are less important than the ends. Adventuresses are *open* women—open to new experiences, open to taking risks and chances, open to uncertainty and unpredictability, and open to competition and challenge. While one might admire their romantic creativity and their capacity for *joie de vivre*, they demonstrate a less admirable *ambivalence about intimacy*. They like closeness with a man as long as it remains stimulating, exhilarating and fresh—as long as it keeps them "in heat"—but they distrust it if it becomes predictable, readily available, and routine. Adventuresses, in short, leave themselves *wide open* for disappointment in love, so wide open, in fact, that a keen observer could wonder whether they enjoy the disappointment phase as much as the adventure phase.

This is a pair who are sure to attract attention when they get to the dance floor. As you will see, they have an eye-catching energy and vitality:

The Adventuress	**The Adventurer**
Her family	*His family*
Distant father/depressed mother	Abandoned son
Loss of parent	Invisible triangle
Disapproving parents	Disapproving parents
Daddy's girl	Mama's boy
Alcoholic father	Alcoholic father

Her profile	*His profile*
She is a compulsive fun lover in rebellious response to an austere, strict father.	He is a compulsive fun lover in rebellious response to an austere, authoritarian parental style.
She is attractive, spunky, competitive, visceral, eager for experience, easily bored.	He is not necessarily handsome, but a good con artist, an experimenter, hyperactive, "pizzazzy."
She is a risk taker, a rule breaker.	He is a risk taker and a rule breaker.
She is ultra-dependent on a man for excitement and stimulation.	He prizes his freedom.
She often has an inherited income or confidence in her ability to make it on her own financially.	He is a career changer, very successful or barely making it financially.
She wants to triumph over his other women and is ambivalent about intimacy.	He clearly prefers adventure to intimacy. He likes playing one woman against another.
She experiments with substance abuse.	He experiments with substance abuse.
She is volatile, easily loses control.	He is volatile, easily loses control.
She is still a kid.	He is still a kid.
She becomes disappointed and despondent when reality sets in and the romantic adventure becomes a routine affair.	He never faces reality.

The relationship dissipates of its own accord without much fanfare on either side, or it continues intermittently and is interspersed with other relationships until it finally withers away.

DIRTY DANCING

The Adventurer's sexuality is on display in every move and step he takes. He's an improvisational dancer, and he invites his partner to be one too. Together they writhe and wiggle, shimmy and shake. They're a risqué pair on and off the dance floor. Off the floor, the Adventurer introduces his partner to a variety of experimental behaviors. These may include nontraditional sexual practices like orgies or ménage à trois experiments, and may be accompanied by alcohol and drug ingestion to remove inhibitions. Mike's story is typical:

"When I was twenty-two, I started dating a group of women. I'd have one main one, but slept with others as well. There were seventeen in all. After I was married, I had one woman who introduced me to Hindu sexual practices. For a short while during my marriage I was faithful, but then I started going to professional conventions, and I began to collect women in different cities who I see whenever I'm in town. Sometimes I go on masturbating binges for long periods of time. People think my sexual escapades are interesting. I'm curious about all forms of sexual experience. I've tried homosexual practices and many forms of group sex. I like to be with intelligent women who are sexually curious and adventurous, and I appreciate it when they understand that there is a difference between sex and love. When I meet women who can make the distinction, the affairs go on and on. Now, I'm something of a legend. People talk about my strings of women."

And so is Jeff's:

> "I'm married to a dull woman. After ten years of marriage, I began seeing call girls for one-night stands. I did this two or three times a month. Sometimes I got involved in ménage à trois arrangements. With call girls I'd use a fictitious name, but intermittently I had longer-lasting affairs. I'd use my real name when I was having an affair. I've fallen for some of the women I've had affairs with, but I never had the guts to leave my marriage."

Sam spoke candidly about the meaning of sex in his life:

> "I do most of my relating through sex. I shoot first and ask questions later. I'm a very physical person. Affairs are over for me when the sexual chemistry fades. I'm not relaxed, and I have to be on the go all the time. I'm rebellious. I like to do what I want to do, not what other people want me to do."

Jack: "I was after sex in all my relationships with women, but I'd make it appear that I was interested in marriage at first. I'd do this with several women at the same time. I'd play this game until they'd catch on. Then, I'd be on my way."

James: I love women's bodies—the discovery, the touching, the sensuality, and the sexuality. It's delicious. I like the whole sexual dance—the mutual seduction."

Because the Adventurer is the most *blatantly sexual* of womanizers, he is the one most likely to experiment with homosexual activity. Here, one could again use Picasso as an example of the Adventurer/satyr whose sexual proclivities direct him toward both heterosexual and homosexual activity. Sex for the Adventurer is the essence of life's pleasure. The Adventurer cannot conceive of living without sexual variety, and if some of the candy at the store is flavored homosexually, he is tempted to try it (assuming that he's rebellious enough to ignore the social stigma).

Even if kinky sex is not part of their mutual repertoire, the Adventurer and the Adventuress will spend a good deal of time in pursuit of new sexual experiences with one another, and are likely to experiment with nonsexual feats of daring as well. He, and maybe she along with him, will drink too much, use drugs too freely, drive too fast, spend money neither of them has or money that he borrows from her, and/or participate in athletic challenges beyond the level of their capability. If either or both of them are married to other partners, they will arrange their trysts in such a way as to endanger their marital and familial relationships. Karen, whom you will recall as the daughter of an alcoholic father and a severely depressed mother, is as good an example of an Adventuress as any woman could be:

> "The womanizers I fall for are all drinkers, so they're loose and uninhibited. They like to party. I drink right along with them. Probably you'd say I have a drinking problem, but I think I can control my drinking. I've been involved with both married and single womanizers, and a few of them have gotten me pregnant. One man I was involved with borrowed thousands of dollars from my trust fund. I had to take him to court. Then I took over his business, turned it around, and got my money back."

The Adventuress and the Adventurer like living on the edge, but nothing they do is closer to the precipice than their own wild involvement with each other. Theirs is a relationship of high drama and intensity. It starts with a bang and ends with a whimper. Typically, the woman in this duo tires first, wears herself out trying to keep up with him and hang on to him, makes attempts to tame him, and finally, when all her energy is spent, leaves him or lets him leave. For him, her loss is not a serious one, because there have been other women all along. Besides, there will be new ones to add to his roster. Sometimes this fast-lane life leads to tragedy—for example, the accidental death of one of them, the suicide of a betrayed spouse, or the development of a toxic addiction by the newly initiated Adventuress.

The Adventuress, like the Princess, is averse to *relationship drudgery*, but she carries the aversion several steps further than the Princess does. Her relationships are not as pretty. Hearts and flowers are replaced by *thrills*, which have an unseemly quality that is apparent from the beginning of the relationship. Alcohol, drugs, marital deceit, sexual free-for-alls, emotional volatility are part and parcel of the romantic package she receives as she begins her roller-coaster odyssey with the Adventurer.

Although *lack of self-esteem* is a characteristic that describes the Bimbo and the Princess, for the Adventuress it's a trademark. Not only does she feel unworthy of respectful treatment from men, *but* she also feels a *lack of selfhood*. "Who am I? Why am I here? What makes me tick?" are questions she can't answer. Romantic adventure is the stimulus she requires as proof of her existence. Without it, she is comparable to a car without a transmission—a body without a vital inner mechanism. Of course, there are gradations of pathology for her as for the Bimbo and the Princess. Call girls and prostitutes are Adventuresses *in extremis*. Most Adventuresses stop far short of the sex-for-sale mark. They draw a moral line at some point before that level is reached, but the line is apt to be lower on the continuum than it would be for most women. In other words, they have an excessive tolerance for bad treatment from men, and unfortunately, the bad treatment frequently serves as the tool to keep the transmission going. Here, Sara reveals how far her adventurous spirit took her in relationships with men:

"When I was twenty-five, my boyfriend told me that I needed more sexual experience, so I picked out one of his friends. This guy told me that he had to have sex every day, and that variety was the spice of life. I went along with the program even though I knew he was sleeping with other women. I did learn a lot about sex and felt powerful with my sexuality. I liked the hot pursuit. I had a dazzling affair along the way with a painter. I took a trip to Europe in the middle of our relationship. He said he would follow me, but he wrote me to say that he'd fallen in love with a fourteen-year-old girl. I got used to bad treatment from womanizers. I was slow to catch on to it."

The Healer and the New Age Narcissist—the Two-Step

This duo is the least noticeable pair on the dance floor and in the popular press. Magazine covers don't display close-ups of them in Hollywood, New York, Paris, or Cannes. Neither photogenic nor flashy, they blend in with their fellow dancers and get lost among the ads, recipes, and beauty tips in the popular women's circulars. The attention they richly deserve is obtained, however, in

professional psychological literature. There they enjoy
some prominence, especially in the parlance of alcoholism where she would be identified as *co-dependent* or
the *enabler,* and he would be identified as the *womanizer* instead of the *alcoholic.*

By transferring the language of alcoholism to the subject of womanizing, I am suggesting that the Healer and
the New Age Narcissist are drawn to one another. Her
talents as an enabler find maximum expression in partnership with him. I use the word "maximum" because
the Healer can be paired with other womanizers as well
as the New Age Narcissist type. Frequently, in fact,
women start out in their relationships with womanizers
as Bimbos, Princesses, or Adventuresses and try to leap
into the Healer role when the going gets rough in their
affairs at the time when they're about to lose their lovers
and aren't ready to let them go.

A woman becomes a Healer in the hope that the gift
of her unconditional love will conquer him. It's an understandable leap, perhaps best expressed by Sylvia when
she said in Chapter II: "I get taken care of, *but I nurture
too in order to keep this type of man for as long as I
want him.*" Understandable as the leap may be, it rarely
accomplishes its purpose. Instead, it becomes the kiss of
death or the coup de grâce to the relationship, because
the Healer, more than her womanized sisters, *assumes
personal responsibility for her mate's behavior and his
pathology.* If she could voice her unconscious thoughts
she would say to her partner: "I understand that your
childhood was difficult and that you have psychological
problems as a result of your upbringing, but I can help
you fix all that. I can make up for your suffering if you
will stick with me. No one can love you as well as I do.
When you begin to see how wonderful my love is, what
good it does for you, you will heal. Then you will want
to leave your other women."

Her kindness and psychological generosity toward him, when he is so undesirous and undeserving of it, allows him to get away with murder. While her *intention* is to keep her man, to nurture him into loving her, her *actions* (the nurturing behaviors) have the opposite effect. They *enable* him or give him permission to continue doing what comes naturally (womanizing).

Unbeknown to her, if the Healer pairs with the Conqueror, the Charmer, or the Adventurer, her message will fall on deaf ears, but if she pairs with the New Age Narcissist it's another story. In the interlude they share together, they speak beautiful psychobabble *until* the day arrives when he decides that as understanding, sensitive, and caring as she is, there's something missing. Somewhere, he hopes, a woman waits for him, one who can love and understand him right down to the core— deep, deep down in a cavern in his soul where no one else has ever entered. Once upon a time he found and lost her, well before he met the woman of the moment. He must look again.

The New Age Narcissistic womanizer has all the makings of a good guy. He appears to have those attributes that contemporary women say they want: psychological awareness, emotional sensitivity, intellect, humor, and modern sociopolitical attitudes about women's rights, health, environmental affairs. Although he's a man of the eighties, he's got a sixties flair. His professional energy is spent in service to the public. Everything is "right" about him with two unfortunate exceptions: (1) his addiction to himself and (2) his inability to cure his old love wounds.

His brand of narcissism differs from that of other womanizers because it is embellished by a keen interest in psychology. To the detached observer (a psychotherapist, for example), he appears as a kind of psychology junkie. He knows the lingo, employs it freely, and finds no subject more worthy of psychological scrutiny than himself. Hard as he tries, though, he can't get over the hurt he suffered when he lost the one true love of his life. (This "lost love" may appear in his conscious mind in the form of a specific, idealized woman with whom he had a relationship, but unconsciously she is a phantom woman, a symbol of a more significant love scar left over from childhood). Marty describes the effect that his "lost love" experience has had on him:

"I don't think I could ever be permanently committed to a woman again because I was so wounded by the one relationship I had that was monogamous. I found her in bed with someone else. To be committed you have to give too much of yourself. I've had a lot of one-night stands. Lots of women have tried to tame me, to help me settle down, but I can't fall into line. Now I tend to go out with women who are unstable. I think maybe I do this because I know it won't work out, and I can avoid commitment."

To the attached observer (i.e., the Healer), a New Age Narcissist is as easily mistaken for an emotionally sensitive man as a love-longing woman is for a love-receptive woman (as described in "The Princess and the Charmer" section). When this type of womanizer relates to a woman, he seems to be in search of her intimate self, *but:*

If the truth could be told, his confession would be;
I looked into you to find more of me.

Since there are never enough reflections of him in any of his female mirrors, and never enough answers to his endless stream of questions about his lovability, he is tireless in pursuit of greener feminine pastures. Ironically, the one kernel of psychological information that he lacks is the one he needs the most. He needs to learn that the prudent application of a little psychology can go a long way, can be life-enhancing and love-enriching, but when it becomes an undirected, obsessional pastime, it can be habit-forming and harmful to a person's mental health—a poor substitute for living, and poorer still for loving.

Guided as much by instinct as anything else, he moves toward the Healer. Her instincts, in turn, tell her that he's her man. She smells his vulnerability, his open wounds, and his receptivity to nurturance. He reeks of emotional availability and sensitivity. She knows how much he needs her, how helpful she can be to him, and how much he will love her in return. Psychologically, and in nine out of ten instances, professionally as well, she is nothing if not a helper. Margaret has the earmarks of the Healer:

"In one of my relationships with a womanizer I recall his telling me that the reason we couldn't have a relationship was because he had so many personal problems, and it wasn't fair for him to impose them on me. He would make me feel that I was special and a threat at the same time. He'd say that other women didn't threaten him as much as I did. This flattered me and got me hooked. I was a good listener, and I tried to help him with his problems, but he went on to other women anyway. Sometimes he'd say that he had to see other women because he had been so hurt by the breakup of his marriage. He was an emotional cripple. I'm a giver. People come to me with their problems. Now I'm learning how to be less nurturing. When my relationship with him ended, I comforted myself by telling myself that he would never forget me. In his heart there would always be a place for me."

The Healer's motto is a simple one: *If you help some-one enough, they will repay you with love.* The New

Age Narcissistic womanizer appears as the best candidate to lend credence to the motto. Through the Healer's eyes, he looks like a man whose cup runneth over with the potions of love, so never mind that the cup has a leak at the bottom. Can we fault her for overlooking the leak? The answer is no. Even the healthiest woman would find him appealing, but she would part from him long before the Healer would. The Healer is attracted to the leak in his loving cup as much as, if not more than, to the ingredients in the cup. The fault, dear Healer, lies not in your oversight but in your motto. Giving help doesn't come with a guarantee for receiving love. On the contrary, it is more likely to yield guilt, shame, helplessness, avoidance, anger, and/or flight.

They dance close together on the floor as if they were glued. She knows just what to do, and he knows how to get her to do it. Both of them have done this dance before with the same kinds of partners. Let me introduce them to you. Their relative inconspicuousness may have caused you to ignore them.

The Healer	The New Age Narcissist
Her family	*His family*
Distant father/depressed mother	Abandoned son
Disapproving parents	The invisible triangle
	Loss of a parent
Her profile	*His profile*
She is attractive, not beautiful.	He is attractive, not striking.
She is nurturing—a giver.	He is needy—a taker.
She is a helper on and off the job, apt to be a social worker, nurse, or other helping professional.	He cares more about liking his work and contributing to society than about financial success.

Her profile	*His profile*
She is outgoing, social, warm, friendly, interested in others, but gullible and easily hurt by people.	He is expressive and analytical about his feelings, somewhat a loner, affectionate verbally and sexually.
She is psychologically oriented, but directs it toward others.	He is psychologically oriented, inwardly directed.
She is moderately sexual, prefers touching.	He uses sex as a salve for his wounds.
She has some addictive troubles with eating and/or smoking.	He is addicted to being understood, but usually feels misunderstood.
She likes to be in control.	He is somewhat undisciplined.
She is *extremely* dependent but looks exactly the opposite.	He is dependent but is afraid of his dependency.
She is self-centered, a martyr; she suffers to keep the relationship intact.	He is self-centered, self-indulgent, exploitative.
She thinks the failure of the relationship is her fault.	He thinks it's her fault too.
She keeps right on helping and giving right to the end, but eventually she burns out when no commitment is forthcoming.	He leaves her or arranges things so that she will leave him.

Before we watch this couple dance, there is a point to be made about dependency as it pertains to the above profiles. The Healer disguises her dependency better than any of the other partners of womanizers. Because she is so capable of taking charge of her relationship, her job, and her living space, she seems self-sufficient, but underneath her helpful, executive manner, she is as needy

as her mate. She longs to be taken care of, but she expresses it by giving care instead. Having given up all
hope of ever receiving care for herself, she settles for the
assurance of a *need to be needed*. When a man stops
needing her, she feels useless and helpless, and if she is
abandoned, she is highly susceptible to prolonged
depression. Sometimes, in order to escape the depression, she will attempt to woo her lover back. Claire confessed that that was her style with womanizers:

> "My pattern was to leave this kind of guy when he
> couldn't deliver a commitment, but afterward I'd change
> my mind and try to reopen the relationship by trying
> to work things out, but by that time the guy wouldn't
> want to talk about it anymore. I'd try to start things up
> again because I'd feel lonely and depressed, and be-
> cause I'd convince myself that it was my fault that things
> went wrong."

The Healer's companion, the New Age Narcissist, is
not nearly as skilled as she is at hiding his dependency,
but he is much more afraid of it than she is. Men, after
all, are supposed to be strong and self-reliant. The more
this type of man comes to rely on a woman, the more
ready he will be to escape her. At the moment when his
dependency becomes apparent to him, he will employ
every tactic in the book to extricate himself from the relationship.

THE TWO-STEP

The dance they do is more predictable, less intricate or
intriguing than the dances performed by the other pairs.
As long as it lasts, both partners think of their dance as
a significant one. In this sense, he is a different kind of

bird from the rest of the womanizer flock. He does not intend to deceive anyone. If he's married, he is very likely to tell his wife about his affair without waiting for her to discover it, and then he may consider the possibility of divorcing her to marry his new beloved. As a single man, he honestly believes that he is available to commit himself to a long-term relationship. He can tolerate longer periods of monogamy than other womanizers can. His womanizing is, usually but not always, *successive* rather than *simultaneous*. The problem, as he sees it, is not so much that he's incapable of commitment (although he does begin to wonder after a number of spins on the merry-go-round), but rather that he hasn't found Ms. Right. If he suspects that he is phobic about commitment, it is usually his last suspicion and is added to his list of self-doubts to be examined under the ever-present psychological microscope. There it is likely to sit for an indeterminate period of time.

Meanwhile, she thinks she can help him come around to an exclusive, permanent attachment to her if she just continues to be patient, understanding, solicitous, and loving. Nothing could be further from the truth. Every two-step she takes forward in the dance sets her back two steps. The Healer is not a risk taker. She doesn't dare change the dance for fear that the relationship will fall out of her control and out of her grasp. There is no mystery about her. She knows what moves she'll make, and so does he. She operates on automatic pilot. In all of her attempts to help him into loving her, she is, step by careful step, helping him to leave her. Sometimes he catches on to the fact that her own agenda (keeping him) is stronger than her love for him. This recognition facilitates his exit.

Strange as it seemed, in several instances I observed that this type of womanizer sometimes identified with the aggressor; that is, he assumed the characteristics of the Healers he had rejected. He started out in his romantic life as a New Age Narcissist, and after a number of relationships with Healers, he became so familiar with their role that he adopted it as his own. Then he would become involved with emotionally unstable women who needed his help more than he needed theirs. When this kind of transformation took place, he would end up as the rejected party in the relationship.

It is easy to detect a melancholic strain in the words of the New Age Narcissist. He fantasizes about a happy relationship with a woman, but never seems to be able to assemble his personal psychology and his desires into a *modus operandi*. Gene, a man in his forties, is a case in point:

> "I was faithful to my second wife. She was the only one I can say that about. I always thought I wanted the Ozzie and Harriet marriage. I believe in monogamy, but I haven't met the right person. I make myself available to unstable, unavailable women. I try to help them, but they betray me. My mother betrayed me for my father, and my first wife betrayed me. I had acute anxiety after the first marriage dissolved. I went to therapy about it years ago. Nothing I've done has brought me what I want—a happy marriage."

So the New Age Narcissist reasons that he's just one of the unlucky ones who was dealt a bad hand in matters of the heart. Nonetheless, it mystifies him that other men succeed in love while he continues to fail. If he suspects that the perfect woman doesn't exist in reality, he doesn't let the suspicion influence his behavior. He persists in looking for her—forever chasing rainbows. To some extent, popular culture spurs him on by promoting the dangerous illusion that he can have it all. Each time he fails to find her, he places another black mark on his lovability score.

Mutual melancholy is the glue that binds this pair. She is sad, too, because she never really succeeds at her mission. God knows how hard she tries, but as many a missionary discovers after years of unceasing effort, it's not that easy to convert people—to make them become what you want them to be. To be a successful missionary means to approach your task without expectations of gratitude or love in return for your work. Healers, however, have high expectations of receiving rewards from their partners. Their stories are sad simply because they give so much, hope for a lot, and receive so little. Joy, that most wondrous of emotions, continually passes them by.

In closing, I want to emphasize that the pairs you have been introduced to on the dance floor do occasionally switch roles and types of partners. Picasso, for example, played all the womanizer roles, sometimes simultaneously, sometimes consecutively, but he was adept at all of them. While most womanizers and their women fall into one dance pattern and stay with it, a few do expand their repertoire so that they can perform more than one or all four of the dances.

PART III

Dancing Lessons

CHAPTER VI

The Same Dance—
Your Choreography

If the golden era for women is the time when they are assured of equal pay for equal work and equal opportunity without fear of sex discrimination, then surely we'd have a consensus that that time has not arrived. We're on our way, but we're not there yet. In the meantime, we live with current realities: We make less money than men do; a small minority of us have risen to the top of businesses, professions, and trades, but the majority of us are lower on the job ladder than men with comparable qualifications; a growing number of us are single-parent heads of households—dependent on alimony and child-support checks, inadequate personal paychecks, or subsistence welfare checks; and many of us are unpaid homemakers without résumés or portfolios to help us compete in the job market should the necessity arise

When we combine our economic gains with our economic realities, we are led inexorably to the conclusion that our economic well-being is still correlated to our relationships with men. Although we don't claim to love them or marry them for their money, we do welcome their donations, and we count on them to sustain whatever life-styles we think we ought to have.

This point was brought home to me, in a poignant way, when I taught adult-education classes for single women. When asked about the criteria that were most important in choosing a potential mate, the overwhelming majority, out of a sample of several hundred women, listed "successful" as one of the top three criteria. Resisting a simplistic and overly judgmental reaction to this finding, I determined that it was not simply gold digging that accounted for the response (although it may have been in some instances), but rather that these women were telling me something about contemporary economic and romantic reality. They were saying that the size of a man's paycheck was an essential component in establishing a climate for love. They had added it up—house, cars, clothes, food, health and fitness, children, college, catastrophic illness, emergencies, and pleasure—and the total came to an impressive number of digits. If these were the things that constituted the right climate, then it was natural for women to seek mates who could provide them (or a hefty share of them). From their point of view, it was impossible to envision love thriving in an atmosphere of privation. Love lasts longer and wears much better on Easy Street than it does on Hardknocks Boulevard.

Despite my attempts to explain that there was very little evidence to substantiate the claim that the prosperous (male or female) fare any better at love than the rest of us do, it was a hard notion to sell to a generation of women raised on the "more is better" creed. Yet, in my

view, affluence is a contributing factor to marital break-
down because it tempts people to take the easy way out
of their difficulties. In the face of inconvenience, dis-
tress, or discomfort, the affluent person has access to quick
remedies. He can buy an air conditioner when he's hot,
fly to Bermuda when he needs a rest, hire a good divorce
lawyer when he grows weary of his wife, and have enough
money left over to woo another woman just to keep his
spirits up.

Womanizing is an avocation that requires outlays of
cash. It costs money to juggle women. Wining, dining,
entertaining, and gift giving come with the territory, so,
as Sylvia said in Chapter II, "Womanizers have money."
Not all of them are rich, of course, and many of them
have wives and children to support, but it's hard to be
poor and sustain a womanizer's life-style. Since so many
women nowadays are seeking monied men, it is not sur-
prising that womanizers have a relatively easy time at-
tracting women on that basis alone. However, we have
already seen that in addition to their career successes,
womanizers come equipped with other assets. They're
fun, charming, challenging, exciting, adventurous,
sexual, romantic, and hard to resist. They appear to
have it all, and on top of that they have you and other
women too.

One little fling with a womanizer might not hurt you,
but what if you're married to one or deeply involved with
one, what does that do to you? What should you do about
it? What are your options? When we arrive at the point
where these questions have to be asked, we can also
question whether life on Easy Street is as easy as it looks.

What Am I in for If I'm Married or Strongly Attached to a Womanizer?

You're in for some heartbreak, especially when you first discover that there is (are) another woman. Women have told me that the moment of discovery was one of the most painful they'd ever endured. Some women arrive at this point with previous suspicions, but many come to it without the slightest suspicion. Either way it hurts, but being totally unprepared for the revelation hurts more. Once the discovery is made, you can expect to experience the following emotions:

1. Extreme sadness

2. Varying levels of anger or rage—at him, at her

3. Jealousy—"What does she have that I don't have?"

4. Self-accusation—"Where did I go wrong?" "What did I do to cause this?"

5. Desire for revenge—"I'll kill him." "I'll kill her." "I'll go have an affair."

6. Action impulses—"I'll call her and confront her." "I'll get in my car and see if I can find her or catch them both."

7. Depression and confusion—"What do I do now?" "What does this mean?"

8. Fear—"What if he leaves me?" "What will become of me?"

The Confrontation

Most women faced with this array of emotions choose to confront their husbands or lovers about his affair(s). (Often, they choose to confront the other woman, too, but this only serves to heighten the intensity of the emotions.) Before discussing the various outcomes that can result from confrontation, let me remind you that womanizing is an *addictive behavior,* so you should not approach confrontation with the idea that once the cat is out of the bag, the behavior will stop. In all but a handful of cases, this is a misguided hope. There may be an interlude of fidelity prompted by his fear that you will now be more vigilant about his activities than you were in the past, but it will last only as long as his addictive impulses allow. Confrontation doesn't stop an addiction, whether it's an addiction to women or a substance addiction. At best, it puts a temporary brake on it.

What then are the probable outcomes of confrontation?

1. He will admit that he's been seeing someone else, stop for a while, then resume the activity.

2. He will admit that he's been seeing someone else, will promise to mend his ways, but will continue unabated.

3. He will admit that he's seeing another woman (women), but he will say that it's your fault that he's doing it. If you were a better spouse or lover, he wouldn't be doing it.

4. He will deny that he's seeing anyone else, blame his wife or the confronting lover for falsely accusing him, and continue womanizing.

5. He will admit that he's been unfaithful and that it's a problem, and he will consent to go to counseling to work on the problem *at his wife's or lover's urging*. Once in counseling, he will decide that it's not helping, and since he didn't really want to change himself in the first place, he will find a way to terminate the counseling.

6. He will either admit or deny it, and ask for a divorce.

YOUR REACTION

1. If he admits his dalliance(s), stops for a while, and then resumes, *you will:*
   stay on the lookout, but feel reassured that he's stopped, because he's home more often.

2. If he admits it, promises to change, but resumes womanizing, *you will:*
   accept his promises and reassure yourself that it was only a temporary, minor infraction, but underneath you will be uneasy about it and will remain suspicious. These feelings will fester beneath the surface.

3. If he admits it, blames you for your inadequacies as a mate, and continues womanizing, *you will:*
   feel depressed and will try to be a better, more responsive and understanding mate—especially in the bedroom.

4. If he denies it, blames you for the unfair accusation, and continues womanizing, *you will:*
   feel guilty for having been suspicious and will walk on eggshells to avoid offending him.

5. If you prod him into counseling, *you will:*
   feel encouraged and hopeful, and will see his

willingness to go as an indication of his real feelings of love for you. You will try to be extra helpful, patient, and understanding toward him.
6. If he asks for a divorce, *you will:*
    feel desperate and will beg him to stay. If he refuses, you will alternate between despondency, rage, and vindictiveness. If he says he'll give it one more try, you will bend over backward to please him.

YOUR BEHAVIOR

In the above reactions, we are seeing how the seeds of co-dependency are sown. (See Chapter VII for more information about co-dependency.) Having followed you as you wend your way through discovery, emotional response, confrontation, and reaction, we can see you setting the stage for an *adaptive behavioral stance.* You are preparing yourself to *deny, downplay, or overlook the problem.* This, in turn, finds you *colluding* with his behavior. By refusing to separate yourself from his problem, you are enabling him to share his responsibility for his behavior with you. You say, "Things will be OK if I just hang in, try to be better, go for professional help with him." He says, "I've got her. No matter how much hanky-pankying I do, she will think it's at least partially because of her, so it's not *my* problem, it's *our* problem." The truth is that you have made only ONE contribution to his problem: YOU BECAME INVOLVED WITH *HIM.* Everything else about your predicament is HIS PROBLEM. He, not you, is the womanizer.

How You Should Behave: The Prescription

Before the confrontation, you are entitled to your range of emotions, but thereafter you have a responsibility to yourself to see both the forest and the trees, and to act according to a realistic perception. To do this may require a settling-down period, so you would be well advised to postpone the confrontation until your head is cooler. (This is a gargantuan task, and I wouldn't fault anyone for being unable to carry it out. The need to discharge the emotion is overwhelming. Still, if you can do it, it's a good idea.)

The first and most important steps to take after the confrontation are:

1. Disengage yourself from his problem.
2. Tell him you recognize that *he* has a problem.
3. State that there is very little that you can do to help him with *his* problem.
4. Make some demands. For example: "I want you to understand that our relationship is threatened if you don't do something about your problem. I want you to stop seeing the other woman (women). I want you to admit that you have a problem, and take whatever measures are required to correct it regardless of cost, time commitment, or inconvenience to your schedule."
5. Say, "I will give you _____ [a time period] to do this. If you do not correct the behavior and demonstrate that you are actively working on correcting it, I will have to consider the possibility of separation."

6. Say, if it is true, "Separation is not my first choice as a resolution of the conflict, but it is one that I will have to consider."

7. Say, "I will not allow you to blame me or denigrate me for your behavior. If there are justifiable complaints that you have about me which are related to our general compatibility, I will address those (as long as you don't use them as the basis for your womanizing)."

8. Say, "Your womanizing places *you* and *me* at risk for contracting AIDS. Since that is a life-and-death matter, I think both of us should take an AIDS test. We should not have sexual intercourse until the results are returned to us, and it is another reason why I have to insist that you cease seeing other women."

9. Behave as if you mean what you say. Stick to your guns.

This is by no means a foolproof formula for success nor does it come with a lifetime relationship guarantee. There are risks inherent in it. He might take you up on your offer to separate, but the chances are equally good that he will do that anyway NO MATTER WHAT YOU SAY OR DO. At the very least, the above prescription preserves your integrity and your self-respect—psychological armament that you will desperately need whether or not a breakup occurs. At the very best, the prescription does *you* and *him* a service, because it pinpoints the problem *accurately,* and helps him focus on its true source. Furthermore, it makes it more difficult for him to *diffuse* the problem, to spread pieces of it around where they don't belong.

In our psychologically oriented American culture, it is common practice to label a variety of social behaviors as "sick," which then stigmatizes them and makes them fair game for some form of "treatment." As womanizing in America comes increasingly to be regarded as "sick" behavior, societal pressure mounts on the womanizer to change his ways. Add the threat of AIDS to his pressure cooker, and you give his female partner(s) more muscle to combat his womanizing habit. In the present-day American climate, women have more power than they realize vis-à-vis their womanizing lovers. The social and psychological winds are blowing in their favor.

These are not the prevailing winds for women in cultures where the practice of womanizing is an acceptable, longstanding tradition, such as Italy, France, Greece, and many Arab nations. The more widespread, sanctioned, and entrenched the behavior is in a society, the less amenable it is to any corrective intervention. If everybody's doing it, and there is no hue and cry from a vocal women's movement or from an influential psychological establishment, then it's not seen as "sick." (As another example of behavior that would be considered both "sick" and "criminal" in America, one could point to the traditional Chinese practice of female infanticide. Even when we take the prevalence of child abuse in America into account, it would be impossible in our society to treat the killing of female babies as anything less than an act of a deranged criminal.)

All The Reasons Why You Won't Want to Take My Advice

Money talks louder than I do, and so does the voice from the heart. It's easy for me to suggest that you should rock your loveboat, but for legions of women, it's a very difficult thing to do. Take Frances as an example:

"I hadn't even finished college when I met Nate. He swept me off my feet. I was so happy to be married, and to be married to *him* was extra frosting on the cake. A few months after we were married, I found out about his first affair. I was devastated. I got him to go to a marriage counselor with me. He never opened up, and he quit after a few visits. There were more affairs, but there were children who came along in between affairs. I confronted him about all the affairs he had that I knew about. He would always admit them, express no guilt, stop womanizing for a while, but then resume again. I loved being married, and I worshiped him, so I kind of swept the affairs under the rug, and besides, what was I going to do to support myself if I left him? I had no career or any background for a career."

Frances's marriage lasted for sixteen years. When it ended, it was he who left for another, much younger woman. Her story is one I've heard from countless numbers of women. Some of them kept their marriages intact by simply "sweeping the affairs under the rug," but most were like Frances, rewarded for their loyalty by their husbands' eventual departure from the marriage.

There can be no hiding the fact that money talks. What's a woman to do if she has children, a mortgage, and no viable way to earn a living, much less a living that enables her to live in the style to which she has become accustomed? What if she's more fortunate and has a career (or the possibility of one), but she's forty or older with children in tow and has enjoyed a two-income existence up to this point. She looks down the road and sees a lifetime of loneliness ahead of her. From her perspective, the good men are all taken, and even if there were a good one available, why would he choose her with her juvenile retinue when he could easily find someone much less encumbered? Either way, the picture looks bleak. She reasons that the husband she's got is better than no husband at all. What if she prizes family solidarity over everything else? Won't she be tempted to content herself with the thought that her mate may stray, but he'll always return home to stay? For the children's sake, won't she persuade herself that loyalty to their father is her motherly duty?

And what if she's married or single and loves the guy or worships him, just as Frances did? Wouldn't she prefer to have a piece of him than none of him at all? Why shouldn't she cast her lot into a basket woven with hope? Isn't it possible that if she's as good a spouse or romantic partner as anyone could be, he will see the folly of his ways and reform himself?

Every one of these questions is good and fair. If you're a woman who has put one or all of them to herself, and you have remained in a relationship, you have already answered the question or questions with the same answer: "I should stay with him." This being so, whether or not you have made the *right* decision is irrelevant. If you have made peace with yourself and with your decision, I will attempt to *influence* rather than *alter* it.

The following advice, then, is specifically addressed to those of you who are *sticking with your men.* In general, however, it's also good advice for women who are considering leaving either their married or unmarried partnership with a womanizer. More than just "good," the advice is "essential," because it is important for you to remember that *even if you don't leave him, he is very likely to decide to leave you at some undetermined time, usually at a moment when you least expect it and are unprepared for the boom to hit.*

Everything You Must Do If You Can't Take the Risk of Leaving Him

1. In the inflationary, competitive, familially damaged society in which we find ourselves today, it doesn't make sense for women to be unprepared to compete in the marketplace. One reason for this is simple: There is a high probability that you will have to support yourself (and very likely some children as well) at some point in your life. Despite Ronald Reagan's declarations to the contrary, there is an inadequate safety net for women in America. The other reason is more complex: A job keeps you busy, fills your time, makes you feel valued, offers you a place to strut your stuff, gives you a sense of security—something to fall back on when the going gets rough. When you know you can work at something, you know you can be part of the mainstream. There is a certain confidence, strength, and self-reliance that you acquire as a member or as a potential candidate for the workforce.

2. Therefore, make sure you are trained for something. If you can't afford to pay for your training, borrow the money or apply for aid. It's an investment that pays off.

3. Build an independent life outside your relationship with a man and outside the confines of your family circle. This can be as singular as develop-

ing a hobby or as diverse as making and spending time with your own friends, taking classes, volunteering, involvement in political or community causes or recreational pursuits.

4. Lower your expectations for what a relationship with a significant other can provide for you. Increase your expectations for yourself and for what you can do for yourself.

5. Refuse to take the blame or the responsibility for your partner's womanizing.

6. Develop reliable friendship and support networks, and put energy into maintaining them.

7. Leave yourself open to new experiences. For example: If you meet men naturally, don't shun them. Make friends with them. It is probable that attention from other men will enhance your self-esteem and change your pessimistic picture about your future romantic possibilities.

8. Be out in the world as much as possible. Force yourself out of the safe haven of your nest. Learn to go places alone.

9. Keep a bank account for yourself, and use it for your needs and your pleasure exclusively.

10. Don't pretend to yourself or to other people that your marriage or relationship is perfect.

Now that we've discussed the various things that you will do, should do, probably won't do, and must do for yourself if you intend to stay involved with a womanizer, let's review what we've learned about the culprits themselves—the womanizers in your lives.

Everything You Need to Know About Womanizers—In a Nutshell

THEY'RE ADDICTS

Womanizers are men who are addicted to women. As addicts, they regard women in the same way that any addict regards the thing that he/she is addicted to. For the womanizing addict, women are a *fix*. He has to have them for whatever ails him. Women, then, become depersonalized in his mind. They are objects rather than individuated human beings. While this fact stands as testimony to the womanizer's disregard for women's "personhood" and individual integrity, the irony is that women are not *mere* objects to the womanizer, they are *vital* objects on whom his survival depends. Without them, he is nothing. *This is the trap that trips so many women.* Sensing how important they are to him, women presume that this means that they are beloved for their personal attributes when in reality they are desired for the services they can provide to him.

It follows, then, that as service providers, any one woman is dispensable simply because there are any number of women who can fill the service bill. For a woman married to a womanizer or for a woman in an unmarried relationship with one, the most important thing to remember is that his addiction is an illness that has nothing to do with her. She didn't cause it; she can't cure it; and the only way she can help him is to make it clear to herself and to him that he owns the illness.

THEY'RE NARCISSISTIC

Womanizers are not self-lovers, they're self-absorbed, self-starved, and self-indulgent. These characteristics, as we learned in Chapter IV, are derivatives of childhood deprivations such as maternal abandonment, parental disapproval, paternal or parental disconnection. The unloved boy begets the love-starved man who sets out on a lifelong journey to reclaim the lost love, but because he was unloved, he is incapable of loving himself. Inept as he is at self-love, all his energy must be expended toward that end at the expense of the more mature task of learning to love others. While everybody else has love to spend on themselves and thus on their loved ones, he is busy building an account. He has none to give away.

Womanizers are like gas tanks. They need regular replenishment. Feeling always as if they're operating on "Empty," they're in perpetual search of elixirs to give them the illusion of being "Full." Their primary elixirs are women, but very often there are secondary elixirs as well, such as alcohol or drug use; workaholism or obsession with prestige, power, and success; or compulsive adventurousness and "sexaholism"—any stimulant that helps them feel alive.

But the womanizer's engine cannot run without women, not because he loves women but because they are the chief suppliers of the *approval* he so desperately needs. Approval is all he knows of love, and all he thinks he needs to know. Love, according to his definition, has nothing to do with building a bond between a man and a woman, but rather it has everything to do with building his ego. "You're wonderful, you're marvelous, you're perfect, you're desirable" are the sweet nothings that he must hear repeated thousands and thousands of times.

Only women are capable of validating his manliness.

Womanizing narcissists care more about their gender appeal than they do about their human appeal. Their lives are spent running from being human out of fear that they will be discovered as the nonentities they believe they are. As long as they have a steady diet of approval from as many women as possible, the easier it is for them to feel "Full." While the approval supply lasts, the pressure to be human is alleviated. Hence, in older womanizers, one sees a kind of melancholic regret which accompanies their knowledge that age is going to win the battle. They sense that their approval ratings are headed for a downward spiral, and as they get closer to staring at the face of death, a hint of fear comes through— perhaps a lingering suspicion that they may have to take that road alone, and that when their psychological autopsies are completed there will be revealed large doses of approval in their blood and nary a trace of love.

"Why do men chase women?" asks the mother played by Olympia Dukakis in the movie *Moonstruck.* "I think it's because they're afraid of death," she says in answer to her own question.

They Have a Way
with Women

"I had a feeling that he was a womanizer, but he made me feel so special that I couldn't resist him. He said everything I wanted to hear." These were words out of the mouth of Caroline, an attractive, just-turned-forty brunette who had been married in her twenties to a womanizer. She had been divorced for seven years. This was her second visit to my office, and she was telling me about her most recent romance. "Something in the pit of my stomach told me he wasn't going to call on Saturday

when he said he would. We had a whirlwind week together, and by Friday I could sense that he was slowing
down. All day Saturday, I wanted to call him, but I sat it
out instead. Sure enough, he never called."

Hers was a symphony I'd heard many times before—
the same theme, just a different variation. Womanizers
play the feminine heartstrings with such finesse that even
a suspecting woman can be carried away by the melody.
When one stops to think about the secrets of their success with women, they're not hard to unravel. First,
womanizers spend inordinate amounts of time in the
company of women. They learn to read female whims,
wishes, and vulnerabilities, and they develop a fine-tuned
sensibility for the idiosyncrasies of the species. Second,
they know how to spot the women who will be the most
receptive to their advances. In almost every instance, they
will select women whose "neediness" is either subtly or
obviously apparent. Third, they will know which but-
tons to push to activate a woman's emotional juices and
deactivate her rational inhibitions. Finally, they will set
off full-throttle signals, knowing that the whirlwind that
is about to begin is guaranteed to lift her above and beyond the humdrum, tiresome little routines of daily existence. A womanizer can take her to emotional peaks
that she can't experience in the office, the studio apartment, or the master bedroom. He has a magnetism, intensity, and romantic savoir-faire that his more stable
brethren lack. The journey to the peak with a womanizer
is a moonglow experience as long as it lasts, but as Caroline's example illustrates, it is always followed by a
precipitous fall into a grim, lonesome valley.

Will He Ever Change?

If a woman has been married to a womanizer for a long time, her moonglow moments with him have become scarcer with the passing years. She may not even remember them. For a long time, she has lived with him in the valley and she has adapted to it. Her life, like the lives of millions of wives, has become intertwined with his in a myriad of other ways. Where once upon a time, she may have been outraged by discoveries of his affairs, now she hardly thinks of them. Maybe she never let herself discover them in the first place. Life goes on. The bills are paid, the house repaired, the children educated and married off. The rhythm is familiar and not very different from that in any long marriage. Women live through worse ordeals.

If she had it to do all over again, would she do it differently? The answer is yes and no. Yes, if she were getting married in the America of the 1980s, because the times we live in do affect the way we behave. When there are no wars and economic disasters to threaten our survival, we can devote more time and attention to our psychological needs and gender prerogatives. Modern women are reexamining their relationships with men and in the process are asking for more from them and offering to sacrifice much less for them. As always, this modernization of behavior begins with the privileged classes and filters gradually down the rungs on the social ladder.

The trend has been aided and abetted by the threat of AIDS, which has appeared on the horizon as a stern warning to the populace to apply sexual brakes or risk sudden and untimely death. In this dual-edged atmosphere of marital liberation and deadly plague, womanizers are unappealing marriage partners.

So, yes, *if* she were a thoroughly modern woman starting over again now, she would do it differently, but no,
she probably wouldn't if she had it to do over again in
the era when she married him. Her young adulthood was
not spent in opportune times for women. Most of us, men
and women alike, are inclined to remain *behind* the times
or in *step* with the times. Very few of us have the courage and stamina to keep *ahead* of the times.

This is a circuitous way of arriving at my main point,
but it leads me naturally to the conclusion that there are
two forces now blowing in the societal wind that could
motivate womanizers to change their ways, and as a result, there is one thing that you as his loyal spouse or
lover can do to help him:

First, the momentum in America is shifting away from
sexual promiscuity back to monogamy and fidelity, and
the shift is being assisted by the combined influence of
the women's movement, the media, and the mental-health
establishment. Womanizing is now an "illness" instead
of a "fashion," and as more womanizers are stung by the
stigma, more of them will be motivated to seek help to
correct their aberrant behavior.

Second, AIDS is a serious, viable deterrent to womanizing, and although many womanizers choose to ignore its dangers or claim to have devised methods to
circumvent it (selection of "safe" partners, use of con-
doms), its prevalence will continue to put pressure on
them to rethink their sexual practices.

Third, you can remind your spouse or partner about
his psychological illness and the potential he has (and
thus passes to you) of contracting a fatal physical illness.
This enables you to remove yourself from his problem
so that you can communicate with him objectively and
rationally. If he's not ready to hear it from you, you can
maximize the opportunities for him to hear it from the

media, read about it, and/or obtain help for it from expert professionals. (As a starter, give him a copy of this book, wrap it attractively, and *wait*. It could be at least one of the straws that breaks the camel's back!)

Some womanizers change of their own accord. As I said in Chapter III, those men who viewed their womanizing as a symptom of a personal flaw were the most amenable to change. Among the men I interviewed, all except one of those who had ceased the practice were single men who had reached the conclusion that their behavior was "sick." Married womanizers seemed to have less at stake than their single counterparts. Their marriages had survived in spite of their behavior. They had the children they wanted, the jobs they desired, and as many women as they could fit into their schedules. In a sense, they were saying, "We have the best of both worlds, so why rock the boat?"

The single men who changed their behavior were a more disgruntled lot. For them, time was running out. Although we have become accustomed to thinking of the "biological clock" as a female phenomenon, I think that there is a timepiece that also ticks for men, but the precise moment when the alarm will go off is not as predictable for them. Usually it happens at some point during that loosely defined time span that we call mid-life, sometime between the ages of thirty-five and fifty-five. The reformed womanizers I met told me that the prospect of being alone for the rest of their lives became less palatable with the passing years, and that once they had recognized that womanizing and the likelihood of aloneness were interrelated, they had the impetus to change.

This was not their only motivation, however. As time went on, dormant feelings of self-disgust were kindled by mental and physical fatigue. The circuitous and frantic pace of their life-styles caught up with them. Womanizing didn't feel good anymore. Peter Trachtenberg, a self-confessed former womanizer and the author of *The Casanova Complex*, offers a vivid portrayal of the feelings that prompted his own recovery:

This finally was the summation of my erotic life. It got so that even as that life slowed and became outwardly more stable, the cycle of desire, triumph and dread accelerated. If I cut down on my sexual partners and tried to stay faithful to them for as long as possible, it was partly in the hope that I could slow down the treadmill whirling inside me. In the last months of that life, I had only to meet an attractive woman to go through the entire cycle in a few moments—longing to fulfillment to uncertainty to panic and disgust, flickering like so many riffled cards while I was still framing my come-on. Those feelings were now compounded by a growing sense of insanity, for I knew that all of them were self-induced. There was no room for a real woman amid the whir of my compulsion. I yearned for something that no woman could give me. I was avenging injuries that no woman had ever dealt me. I was living a life whose sole attraction was the fact that it was familiar, as prison is familiar to the convict. None of which, in itself, was enough to make me stop, until it was a question of stopping or killing myself.[1]

CHAPTER VII

A Different Dance— My Choreography

Let's say that you found yourself on the dance floor in Chapter V and that after reading Chapter VI, you've decided that you want to learn a different dance. Maybe you're ready to try some new steps: A-one, a-two, a-three—let's go!

Six New Steps

STEP 1: THE OATH

Repeat out loud to yourself: "I got myself into this dance I've been doing with the womanizer(s) in my life. I will take full responsibility for my participation. I will no longer blame him (them) or anybody else for my misfortunes in love."

STEP 2: THE BIOGRAPHY—LINKING
THE PAST
TO THE PRESENT

With pen and paper in hand, write:

MY FAMILY SYSTEM

Distant Father/Depressed or Martyred Mother _____

Daddy's Girl/Mother's Rival _____

Oppressive Father and Mother _____

Loss of a Parent _____

Other (for example: Alcoholic parent, Ill Parent _____

Fill in these blanks with a fairly thorough description of each of your parents, their behavior toward each other, toward you, and toward your siblings.

Recall:
The effect that your parents had on you.

Any pathological behavior. For example: sexual or physical abuse of you, your siblings.

How you coped with their behavior toward you and toward other family members.

Describe:
The connections you can see between your life as a child and your adult love life. (See Chapter II for guidelines.) Examples:

Your present relationship with your parents. What unfinished business you think you have with each of them.

Your adult love relationships and how you think they connect to your childhood experiences and to your unfinished business with one or both of your parents.

STEP 3: THE LABEL

Keep pen in hand and make check marks in the book at the descriptions that apply to you. Be sure to be brutally honest. Complete every category, and don't worry if you have checks under each of them.

You Are a Bimbo if:

- You let men lead you around _____
- You make few demands on a man _____
- You accept gifts, favors, promises, invitations without asking questions about his intentions _____
- You are attracted to a man because he is important, powerful, mature, rich, successful, authoritative _____
- You are young, beautiful and/or glamorous, and you combine these traits with a desire to be taken care of by a man _____
- You are a dependent person. You believe that you can't have the good things in life without a man to provide them for you. You haven't converted interests, talents, or professional goals into a self-reliant, self-fulfilling life-style _____
- You are ready, willing, and generous sexually _____
- You protest too little about his other women _____

You are a Princess if:

- You're a romantic, a believer in hearts and flowers and the significance of sexual chemistry _____

- You're independent in all facets of your life except your relationships with men. You are smart, well-educated, socially confident, successful in your career. You make enough money to support yourself, but when Mr. Wonderful comes along, you become a wimp
  _____

- You have a strong need to feel special to a man. You fall easily for flattery and attention _____

- You like mysterious, secretive men with lots of charm
  _____

- You pride yourself on your intimacy skills—warmth, curiosity about him, your ability to make him happy
  _____

- Nice, solid, steady men bore you. You like the challenge of winning an elusive man _____

- You fall madly in love _____

- You're a mourner long after the relationship ends __

You're an Adventuress if:

- You like thrills in relationships, highs and lows, experimental, nonconforming, risk-taking behavior __

- You're a rebel versus family, society, norms _____

- You don't feel like a whole person. By yourself you're bored _____

- You're a compulsive fun lover. You like feeling like a kid _____

- You don't worry much about the feelings of his other woman (women) while you're in a relationship with him. You do expect or hope to triumph over your competition _____

- You have mood swings. You're volatile. It's hard for you to maintain a consistent temperamental posture

  _____

- You're self-sufficient on the job. You know how to make it financially or you have independent means to do so _____

- You need an exciting man to get your adrenaline going

  _____

You're a Healer if:

- You spend a lot of time helping others with their problems _____

- You play the role of nurturer and caretaker to your mate _____

- You have a strong need to be needed, to be indispensable _____

- You believe that you can change someone with your love _____

- You need to control people and events _____

- You are addicted to relationships. You will do almost anything to keep a man. You take on other peoples' feelings and problems as if they were your own ____

- You don't know what you feel, and you don't know where you leave off and someone else begins. You're psychologically confused _____

- You have other addictive problems: smoking or eating

  _____

- You are very concerned about what other people think of you _____

- You are self-centered. You believe that anything that happens to the man in your life or the other significant people around you has happened because of something you did _____

- You are other-directed. Life's meaning comes from outside of you. What you feel, think, or see is not as trustworthy or important as that which others feel, think, or see _____

Of course, people cannot be fitted into neat, tidy slots; human beings are too complex for easy quantification. The odds are better than even that you will have found some characteristics in each category that apply to you. You may have been a Bimbo at one time in your life and a Princess at another, or right now you could be a Bimbo with a streak of the Adventuress in her. In other words, it is possible that you are not a 100 percent pure Bimbo, Princess, or Adventuress, but I think it is unlikely that the same can be said if you have checked most of the items on the Healer list. The Healer is a very specific personality type, whose characteristics are interwoven in such a way that it would be difficult to check one item in her category without checking most, if not all, of the others. This is not to say, however, that you may not have converted, at some point on your romantic journey, from a Bimbo, Princess, or Adventuress to a Healer, but the conversion does not seem to take place in reverse. Once you're a Healer, you're always a Healer. Otherwise, you're a recovered Healer.

The value of this checklist is not necessarily its ability to peg you with perfect precision (although it is helpful to you to get as close as possible). It will have done its job if it serves merely as an indicator. If you check all or most of the items in one category, the clustered effect will pinpoint you easily. If you have check marks scattered throughout, it will be more difficult to assign a label to yourself. As a rule of thumb, I say that if you have 5 to 10 or more check marks distributed among the categories, you qualify for admission to the danger zone as a womanizer's partner. More than 10 check marks mean that you have already entered the zone. What is important, then, is not so much what type you are, but the fact that you are endangered. Without doing an injustice to you, we can safely leave some questions about your precise diagnosis unanswered.

STEP 4: THE SYNTHESIS

With your biography in hand, along with the specific (or general) label that you have assigned to yourself, review Chapters I and II. Append your notes with pertinent information from these chapters. Here are two slightly altered real-life examples to use as models:

Jennifer, Single, Age Twenty-Eight

I had a distant father and a depressed mother. I wanted my father's attention, but he never seemed to have time for me. Outside the family, he was affable, charming, well-liked. I was sad about my father's inattentiveness, but I couldn't talk to my mother about it. She was too wrapped up in her own problems. I felt lonely throughout my childhood.

When I came of dating age, I honed in on the boys who were popular and played hard to get, boys who were kind of like my father. I guess you could say that I've continued this pattern into adult life by choosing men who were charming and elusive. I did well in school and landed a good job out of college. I've been successful in my career so far.

My last hearthrob was Chuck. I met him when I was twenty-five. For the first few months of our relationship, he showered me with attention, and made me feel so special. It was so romantic. I was gaga over him. Almost as soon as I let him know how much I really cared for him, he began pulling away from me, but it took me awhile to catch on to the connection. He became increasingly elusive until he finally announced that he was involved with another woman. I fell for his charm, his "fun" side, and made excuses for his elusiveness. It's been two years since we broke up, and I still haven't gotten over him. Other men I've dated since seem boring and dull in comparison to Chuck. I'm trying to win back Daddy. Obviously, I'm the Princess type.

Clara, Married, Age Thirty

I was twenty-two when I met David. He was twenty-six, and I could tell that he'd been around. He knew how to have fun. We'd do exciting things on the spur of the moment like driving to the next state to go to the movies or suddenly deciding to drive into Manhattan to disco-hop, and have a contest with each other to see which one of us would wear out first. Sex with him was terrific. There would always be something new. Life with him sure was a lot more fun and fast-paced than anything I'd experienced before.

My family life was boring, restrictive, and routine. Nothing I ever did was right in my parents' eyes. My father was strict. I wasn't allowed to date in high school. When he laid down the law you had to obey or he'd be mean. He drank. My mother went along with whatever he said. When I left home I was determined to make up for lost time. That's why David was so appealing. He introduced me to fun and excitement. When he asked me to marry him, I was thrilled. My parents didn't approve, but that didn't bother me much. Eloping with him was another adventurous experience for me. After the wedding, we kept up our life-style for several years. David began drinking more and more and I was getting a little tired of being on the go. If I refused to go along with him on his sprees, he'd sometimes go by himself and come home late at night, and eventually, started staying out all night. When he did come home after work, he'd be critical of me, and would blame me for everything and anything.

Things got really bad when our son was born. David withdrew more than ever. It got so we never saw each other. I was burning out. I suggested marriage counseling and told him if he didn't change our marriage was in trouble. He wouldn't go for help, but he said he'd try to change, and for a while he did, but now he's back to his old ways again. I'm sure he sees other women. I don't feel much for him anymore. I'm looking into a divorce, but I'm not sure how well I'll do on my own. There's no question about it—I'm the Adventuress type. I've been a real rebel against my family, especially my father. What's funny is I tried so hard to go against my father, and my husband seems more like my father every day with his drinking and his criticism. I feel like I'm back at Square One.

Now comes the hard part. Like Jennifer and Clara, you've completed your assignment. You've taken the oath, written your biography, given yourself a label, and assembled your data. If your biographical vignettes are anywhere near as problem-laden as Jennifer's or Clara's, you will be asking, "Now, what do I do?"

STEP 5: THE PLAN

Decision time has arrived. If you turn your attention back to The Oath step, you will see that one door has been shut. You can no longer obtain relief by blaming. You, and only you, can assume responsibility for the course of your *past, present, and future* love life. Below is a list of decisions that you will have to make:

1. Do I want to change my behavior with men? Am I prepared to take the consequences of the decision—the possibility that my current relationship with a womanizer may end; the possibility that I may have to endure periods of depression, loneliness, confusion; the risk of abandoning the known for the unknown?

2. Do I want to shoot for the moon and try to do a complete overhaul of my romantic repertoire or would I prefer a piecemeal approach?

3. Am I willing to make the investment in time, energy, and possibly money that changing my behavior may require?

To help answer the above three questions, ask yourself: What are my priorities for now and for the future? Here is a list of probable priorities for you to rank. The number "1" represents the highest priority and the number "11" the lowest priority:

a. Success in my career _____

b. Being single and remaining single _____

c. Having a stable, long-term, monogamous marriage _____

d. Having a child or children as a single person _____

e. Having a child or children with a man _____

f. Having material possessions _____

g. Having unlimited freedom to do as I please _____

h. Having relationships with men without strings attached _____

i. Living with a man without being married _____

j. Self-growth, increased self-awareness, self-reliance

_____ _____

k. Just being married regardless of husband's erratic
   behavior_____

The way you rank your priorities will tell you a lot
about yourself, and will assist you in making the above
decisions. Obviously, if you rank "c" as your highest
priority, you will be more motivated to change your self-
defeating behavior with men than you will be if you rank
"a," "b," "d," or "k" as your number-one priority.

Having taken this detour, let's return to the decision list:

4. What resources are available to me should I choose
to work on changing my behavior?

The Self-Help Method with the aid of books, magazines, leaderless support groups, or a program that you
devise yourself.

Professional Counseling: Psychiatrists, psychologists,
social workers, public and private mental-health agencies, social-service and family-counseling agencies, sec-
tarian and nonsectarian counseling services, therapy
groups, professionally led groups for Women Who Love
Too Much.

No-Fee Specialty Services: Al-Anon, Alcoholics Anonymous, Sex Addicts Anonymous, Adult Children of Alcoholics Groups (some are fee-based), peer groups for
Women Who Love Too Much.

5. How do I determine which resource(s) is right for
me? This is a hard question for me to answer, and harder
still for you. Nonetheless, there are some general guidelines:

Your personal resources make a difference. If you can
afford professional services or have insurance coverage
for them, you will be more likely to avail yourself of the
opportunity, but you should be aware of the fact that there
are low-cost services available. There is no correlation

between the amount that you pay and the quality of the service you receive, but there may be minor inconveniences in selecting a public mental-health, social-service, or family-counseling agency over a private practitioner. Examples would be waiting lists, caps on the number of visits allowed, or geographical distance.

It may make good sense to *avail yourself of several services simultaneously,* perhaps a peer support group along with individual therapy or any other combination of the services I've listed above.

Some components of The Self-Help Method will be necessary whether or not you choose to take the professional-help route. As far as I'm concerned, the more you do for yourself the better, so long as you know when you've reached an impasse and are willing to solicit the help of a professional. In my practice, I am very apt to see love-addicted women on a monthly rather than weekly basis, with a heavy dose of assignments in between sessions. I also encourage the use of resources other than myself. (As someone who has led time-limited groups for love-addicted women, it is my habit to encourage the group to meet regularly on their own after my involvement has terminated.)

If you come from an alcoholic family system or have addiction problems yourself, the Al-Anon and Alcoholics Anonymous and the Adult Children of Alcoholics groups are essential. This also applies to Adult Children of Abusive Parents. Now in most communities there are free support groups for this population. In the Adult Children groups, the definitions of Alcoholic and Abusive Parents are often very loose so that they are appropriate services for people who come from "dysfunctional" families where alcohol and physical or sexual abuse were not the primary source of the dysfunction.

If you come from a "dysfunctional" family as I described it in Chapter II, or as Robin Norwood defines it in *Women Who Love Too Much, some kind of professional help or a consistent support service is a sine qua non for recovery.*

Because the relationships between you and your womanizer(s) are addictive, *professionals who are knowledgeable about the addictive process may be better bets for you than many traditionally trained, psychodynamically oriented therapists.* In this regard, the low-cost or no-cost services are often more effective than more expensive private psychotherapists. The mental-health establishment, in my view, has been slow to appreciate the prevalence of addictive love problems and is, therefore, often ill equipped to diagnose and treat them. Professionals who specialize in the relatively new field of Co-Dependency (an offshoot of the alcoholism and chemical-dependency specialties) are well qualified to deal with love-addiction problems. Two of the tenets of Co-Dependency theory that make infinite sense to me as a way of viewing and treating any addictive disease (including love addiction) are that:

- Co-Dependency is a disease in itself. It's not simply the alcoholic, the womanizer, or the substance abuser who is ill, but the significant others in his/her life who are involved with him/her *because* they suffer from a separate illness (Co-Dependency). By this definition, the Healer is not the only Co-Dependent among the womanizer's partners. The Bimbo, the Princess, and the Adventuress are Co-Dependents too. Co-Dependency, like alcoholism or womanizing, requires a specific treatment approach.

- The treatment should include the Twelve-Step Program that Alcoholics Anonymous utilizes for the treatment of alcoholics, and should provide Co-Dependents with ample exposure to other Co-Dependents so that they can learn from one another in the recovery process.

Now that you have a list of helpful hints to facilitate the decision-making, the final selection of a course of action (or nonaction) rests with you.

STEP 6: THE PROGRAM

Once you have chosen a treatment program for yourself, you will need to follow some basic rules:

1. Make a wholehearted commitment to it.

2. Give it a period of time to take effect. Remember that much of its effectiveness will depend upon your active, consistent participation in the process. The more of yourself you put into it, the more you will receive from it.

3. The decision does not have to be irreversible. If you honestly feel that you have contributed effort and time, and still there seems to be a lack of forward motion, you may want to alter the whole program or those parts of it that aren't working for you.

4. Don't expect change to happen overnight, even under the best of circumstances. These kinds of co-dependent love addictions are so entrenched that they often require extensive help before recovery comes. There are no quick fixes.

CHAPTER VIII

Dancing Teachers—Their Choreography

In my opinion, there are two kinds of experts. The first kind earns the title through study and on-the-job experience in a particular field of endeavor. The second kind earns the distinction through life experience. Each of them has a unique contribution to make.

As a practicing psychotherapist, I have read enough books, clocked enough client hours, and lived long enough to qualify as an "expert" in my field. Like most of my colleagues, I've also had enough struggles, hurts, and triumphs of my own to enable me to feel empathy for other people. But no matter how empathetic I may be, it's nonetheless true that I haven't walked down all the corridors in my clients' or my readers' lives. I have had enough personal experience with womanizers, however, to know something of what it feels like to be involved with them. They, along with other kinds of men, appear on the pages of my own romantic-history book, but those experiences represent old pages rather than new chapters in my biography.

For this book, then, I want readers to hear from the other kind of "experts"—women whose biographies are chock-full of fresh, front-line experience with womanizers. Some of them are married women, some divorced, some single. They range in age from thirty to sixty-five. Some have been introduced to you in previous chapters. Others are new voices. Together they form a chorus of experts. To all of them, I put the question "What lessons have you learned from your relationship(s) with the womanizer(s) that you think are important to pass on to other women?" Here, then, are the answers from the mouths of women who've had experience with womanizers.

Stop, Look, Listen, and Ask

STOP! Read carefully: "BEFORE I KNEW WHAT WAS HAPPENING, HE'D SWEPT ME OFF MY FEET." Read it again and make sure you've digested it thoroughly, because that's where the trouble begins, and you're not going to let that happen to you. You're going to know what's happening before you get entangled with him, and you're not going to allow him to treat you like a tornado would. So you're going to start right off by slowing things down. You're going to ask for time out. Then you're going to behave just the way the people do who work in those storm-control centers. You've turned on the caution light, now you . . .

LOOK! at these words: "I WISH I HADN'T *OVER-*

LOOKED SO MANY THINGS ABOUT HIM." Those are the words of regret that almost every woman utters if she's been involved with a womanizer, but you're not going to have to say them. Remember, you're sitting in the lookout tower. Susan was your predecessor on the job, and she's posted a list of danger signals for your convenience:

1. Watch out if he's *too* nice at the beginning of the relationship.

2. Watch out if he seems to have a strong need to be in command all the time.

3. Watch out if he doesn't share information about himself or about his comings and goings.

4. Watch out if he's not available at critical times.

5. Watch out if he seems averse to tackling real problems.

6. Watch out if he's blaming *you* for *his* inadequacies.

7. Watch out if he shows signs of being an alcoholic, a workaholic, or a success-driven personality.

8. Watch out if he looks too good to be true, because that probably means he's hiding something, and that something is very likely to be his other women.

Women who wished they'd stayed longer on the job in the lookout tower repeatedly emphasized how important it was to STAY ALERT, PAY ATTENTION, AND REFUSE TO OVERLOOK ANYTHING ABOUT THE GUY. Meg said, "It's hard to be that disciplined when you're in a state of passionate attachment. You have to force yourself to be detached enough to look, but if you do it, you can save yourself a lot of heartache." And that's not all. You have to . . .

LISTEN! to this: "I TOOK WHATEVER HE SAID

AT FACE VALUE, AND I IGNORED ANYTHING I DIDN'T WANT TO HEAR." These are intelligent women speaking, but listening skills are not automatic by-products of intelligence. You have to cultivate the ability to listen, and there are two people you have to listen to—you and him. So, prick up your ears, and listen to Sara:

> "Make a vow that you will find a way to tell if he is telling you the truth or not. You have to have the truth. Maybe he will have lost the ability to tell the truth to himself, never mind to you, so you will have to go looking for it. If he doesn't know his own truths or he's just plain deceitful, he won't be able to tell you the truth. You will have to figure this out about him *before* he makes a fool out of you or breaks your unsuspecting heart."

Sara is preparing you to listen for clues from him. Here are some of them:

1. He's evasive. He doesn't give direct answers to questions.

2. He relies heavily on flattery as a communication tool.

3. His words and his behavior don't match.

4. He doesn't see problems where you *know* they exist.

5. He uses the "I'm a lost soul" pitch to arouse your sympathy and your maternal instincts.

6. He tells you, either directly or indirectly, that he's a womanizer.

His is not the only voice you have to listen to. You also need to hear yourself talking to yourself. Take Elaine as an example:

"Early on, when you get a tug in your stomach, pay attention to it. Don't pass it off as something minor. It's probably a small indication of a big problem. Even something as slight as his getting up to get himself a cup of coffee and not asking you if you want one can mean something. The womanizer in my life was a very self-centered person, but I was always making excuses for him such as: "He's not really a self-centered person, he's just that way because he had a difficult divorce." Or I'd say, "It doesn't really mean anything when he says he's a womanizer. When he gets to know me better, he won't be one and he won't say he's one." Even when he told me the truth I didn't listen. I was post-divorce myself when I met him, and I just wanted somebody to be there so I wouldn't be lonely. That's why I didn't pay attention to what he said and who he was. If I had confronted him, and said, "Knock it off," maybe we could have had a chance as a couple. I'll never know, but I think that's what women should do."

Elaine then went on to a subject that every woman should pay attention to, but especially women who are feeling vulnerable about loneliness:

"If you know what you're dealing with, an affair with a womanizer can be a pleasant interlude in your life, but if you put your heart and soul into a relationship with one and overlook his true colors, you'll wind up hurt. The worst thing to do is to allow yourself to think in *forever* terms. You can expect to have fun, but you can't expect much more than that."

Jill says:

"With womanizers you are always faced with a bag of mixed emotions. You have strong feelings that propel you toward the person, but behind those there are always some disquieting feelings. It's just that you don't listen to them. You don't want to hear the voices inside that are telling you to move away from him, but in the long run those feelings usually turn out to be the more important ones."

Jill had some examples of conflicting emotions that she'd experienced with the womanizers in her life:

1. He's so much fun to be with, but it bothers me when I think he's had too much to drink.

2. I love the way he is when he's with me, but I wish he wasn't so busy.

3. I like it that he seems so sure of himself, so capable of handling every situation, but I wish he'd ask me for a little input now and then.

4. I like the fact that he's so popular with other people, but sometimes I feel uncomfortable when he's talking to another woman.

Now, Jill says, "If only I had listened to all the feelings that came after the word 'but' instead of all the ones that came before it." How right she is, and the more so because second thoughts are frequently more grounded in reality than first thoughts are, and therefore are more reliable aids for good decision-making in general and good romantic decision-making in particular. *But* you won't be able to listen to him or to yourself very effectively if you don't . . .

ASK! "I DIDN'T ASK HIM FOR ANYTHING I WANTED OR NEEDED. I THOUGHT THAT I WAS LUCKY JUST TO HAVE HIS COMPANY AND WHATEVER ATTENTION HE COULD GIVE TO ME. I DIDN'T EVEN ASK HIM WHAT HE WAS DOING WHEN HE WASN'T WITH ME." Again, we hear the voice of regret, but now it sounds more plaintive, as if the speaker is bewildered by her own negligence, as if she is asking herself, "How could I have been so stupid?" Listen to Emily:

"I was married for nine years. I was naïve and inexperienced. It took me four years to catch on that my husband was womanizing. I didn't start questioning him about it until the last year of the marriage. I just didn't think husbands did this sort of thing. Finally, I confronted him and said that I thought he was seeing other women. He said there was something wrong with me, and that I should go for help. He'd tell our friends that I was looking at other men. He blamed everything on me. Looking back on it, I think I overlooked what he was like because I wanted our marriage to appear perfect. I liked things to go well. I even downplayed the fact that after two years of marriage, he lost interest in our sexual relationship. Later, I realized that he had put me on a pedestal. I was the Madonna, and his other women were the whores."

Emily is now happily remarried. Her former husband has been married twice since their divorce. She learned two invaluable lessons:

"When you ask your husband or lover the hard questions, if the answers are evasive, if he tells you it's your problem and accuses you of prying, that means something. Responses that don't seem right aren't right.

"If you don't have communication on all levels—sexual, intellectual and emotional—it's going to be very difficult to have it at all. Maybe, if you go for help together early in the relationship, something can be done about it, but even that doesn't come with a guarantee."

June, an attractive, accomplished woman in her early thirties, played the Madonna role with many womanizers until very recently, when she finally realized that none of these relationships had any substance. Like Emily, she never asked for much from men:

"Most of the time with these men, I knew what was going on. I knew they were seeing other women, sandwiching them in when they weren't with me, but I couldn't bear the idea of being abandoned so I didn't say anything. They were all handsome, charming overachievers—men who had risen from humble beginnings to the top. They saw me as a challenge. They used their best techniques with me. I looked great. I had a beautiful apartment, good looks, and a good job. Put me with one of them, and we looked like a cloud-nine couple, but underneath I was nauseated most of the time. I was repressing my suspicions about their other women. It was a matter of avoiding the monster. I was too busy trying to please them to concentrate on their personal defects, but all of them had defects—alcoholism, workaholism, excessive ambitiousness. It wasn't until I'd been through five of these relationships that I learned how to abandon them rather than allow myself to be abandoned. With the sixth womanizer, the minute I discovered that he had other women, I broke up with him."

June was able, with the help of a therapist, to cease her fruitless involvements with womanizers. Now she says that the only way she thinks women can overcome these fatal attractions is to "work on themselves."

Develop Yourself

CAREERS

"IF I HAD BEEN TRAINED FOR SOMETHING, IF I'D HAD A CAREER, I WOULDN'T HAVE BEEN SO DEPENDENT ON HIM." This is the persistent refrain one hears from women who were married to womanizers before the women's liberation era widened the career doorways for women. The refrain is always followed by the obvious rhetorical question: "I HAD NO MONEY AND NO WAY OF EARNING ANY, SO WHAT WAS I GOING TO DO IF I LEFT HIM?" As Mary says:

"Modern women are career oriented. They can afford to be independent, but I was raised to get married and have children and that's all. I was totally dependent. When my husband's womanizing and maltreatment of me destroyed our marriage, when I no longer could stand the harassment I received from him and from some of his other women, I went to a lawyer and got a restraining order against him. He finally left. I'm still dependent on him financially, however. I can't remarry because I'll lose my alimony if I do, and I can't support myself in the style to which I've become accustomed."

The younger, more modern women about whom Mary speaks would take issue with some of her assumptions. They would say that careers, in and of themselves, don't necessarily guarantee psychological independence. June, the woman introduced above, is a case in point. She had a good job, but it wasn't enough to counteract her psychological dependency. She says:

"We women are trained from birth to find ourselves through our relationships with other people. We're always trying to please our mothers, our fathers, or the other important people in our lives. That becomes more important than pleasing ourselves. My mother told me once that I was everything she always wanted to be, and my father said he was proud of me because I became a doctor. If everything looked good on the surface, then my parents would be proud of me. When I was with this handsome womanizer or another one, I figured all the approval I got meant that I was doing everything right. As the daughter of an alcoholic, it was always very important to me to have things look right."

Still, Mary is correct in saying that having a career is like having money in a savings account. When the marital monsoon begins, a woman with a career has something to fall back on.

Laura, now in her late thirties, came to "modernity" through the back door rather than the front door:

"Intellectually I was a woman's liberation advocate before my divorce, but after it I was for it in a much bigger way than I'd ever been before. It helped that I had a career to fall back on, but it certainly wasn't going to enable me to bring in an income which was anywhere near as high as that which my husband provided. In my opinion *women get much too hung up on financial security, and it keeps them in bad marriages much longer than they think. Material comfort isn't worth the sacrifice of your mental and physical health.*"

The fact that Laura had a career was a factor in her decision to divorce her womanizing husband, but it wasn't the deciding factor. She, along with countless numbers of women, remained in her marriage longer than she wanted to for fear of losing the level of financial security that marriage afforded her. It was only when she recognized that she could live more happily on less that she was able to leave her husband.

Nonetheless, the knowledge that a woman can be self-supporting goes a long way toward helping her break out of a self-destructive dependency pattern, but it is only one piece of the dependency pie. It has to be supplemented by . . .

SELF-ESTEEM

Careers are one slab in the building of self-esteem, but the biggest contributor to its construction is you: "YOU HAVE TO DEVELOP ALL OF YOURSELF. YOU CAN'T EXPECT A MAN TO DO IT FOR YOU," say all the "experts" in unison, who then go on to say that avoiding this crucial "growing-up" step leaves you wide open for heartbreaking liaisons with womanizers. Here, Jill describes what she thinks women need to do in order to develop self-esteem:

"Women need to have careers that make them feel that they're using their best skills to contribute to the world. They need to care about other people, and care about themselves at the same time. They have to know their own feelings and needs, and be able to give voice to them. If they can do this, they won't tolerate bad treatment from men. They won't be easily dismissed or devalued by men."

Julie puts it this way:

"The womanizer's biggest victim is the woman who can't be alone. She's trying to get self-worth through him that she can't get for herself. The best thing for her to do is use her twenties to be independent, to learn all about herself. It's not a good time to rush into marriage."

Now comes Barbara with her self-esteem formula:

"I was bulimic, and bulimia for me is a metaphor for the self-esteem problem that women who get entangled with womanizers have. They like to be hungry even though it makes them miserable and uncomfortable. They need to find a healthy way to fill themselves up—physically, mentally, and spiritually. Otherwise, they'll go for womanizers who will constantly keep them hungry. The best way to fill yourself up is to develop your creative skills. I think that there's a connection between creativity and addictions, including love addictions. Creative women seem to fall for womanizers, because they think that the chaotic life that womanizers offer will enhance their creativity, that it will teach them spontaneity, originality, and emotional expressiveness, but that's an illusion. You're the only person who can develop your own skills, and when you pair yourself with a womanizer you're trying to come by your talents vicariously."

And back again to Emily:

"After my divorce, I went back to college. It was the greatest thing I could have done. I had to write a lot about myself, and I'd never done any deep self-examining. I got the chance to know myself for the first time."

And finally there's June again who puts it all in perspective:

"I was so busy trying to please everybody that I didn't have the slightest idea who I was. One of the most important discoveries I made was that I still believed in relationships. They're the icing on the cake, but my own experience and that of most of the women I know leads me to the conclusion that women don't want to cook their own cakes. They sit around like a bunch of batter waiting for a man to complete them and cook them, and of course they don't turn out very well."

These women are telling you that one half of the intimacy equation is knowing, loving, and caring for yourself. The other half is him and how well he knows, loves, and cares for himself. Womanizers, they say, are low scorers on the intimacy scale.

Learn What Intimacy Isn't

"I THOUGHT HE LOVED ME, BUT . . ." Here, I can leave it to my readers to fill in the blanks after they've heard from some members of my panel of experts:

Julie: "I thought he loved me, but intimacy to a womanizer means the loss of power and ego. Intimacy is not a word in a womanizer's vocabulary. His philosophy is: *There's too much of me to give to only one woman.* The size of his ego is incredible."

Jessica: "I thought he loved me, but I didn't understand how terrified of intimacy he was. He had all those women to prevent him from being intimate with me. The more women these kinds of men have the less they have to be intimate."

Lauren: "I thought he loved me, but I found out that just because he was sweet in the beginning of our relationship and generous with his money throughout, it didn't mean that he could be intimate. He was a closed person, really. He couldn't talk to me about anything."

Other women on the panel talked about how easy it was to confuse *excitement* with *intimacy:*

Barbara: "I remember the surge of excitement I would get when I hadn't seen one of my womanizing lovers for a while. We'd exchange lustful glances in one moment and in the next we'd be frantically ripping each other's clothes off and making love on the floor. Before I decided to marry my husband, I had to grieve for the loss of excitement that comes with genuine love. Real love is much calmer, but it took me a long time to understand that and even longer to stop missing the excitement stuff. You have to have *balance* in your life to be intimate with another person. Womanizers lack balance. They function in extremes. They're consumed by one thing or another—women, liquor, work, or their own egos."

Amy: "There's no feeling quite as powerful as the lure of the challenge that womanizers present to you. In one massive sweep of the emotions they make you feel hungry, angry, jealous, ecstatic, sad, weak, strong, desirous, desirable, and delirious; all at the same time. All the novels you've read and the movies you've seen tell you that this is what love is. Of course it's not true. Intimacy can't flourish in a field of such high intensity, because intimacy is all about getting to know one another, and that process requires emotional and physical consistency and quiet space over a long period of time."

Sara: "The one good thing that I can say about my experience with womanizers is that it showed me that I was 'open'—open to learning, open to experiencing life. I hope I'm always an open person. It may be that because my openness exposed me to being made a fool of and being hurt by womanizers, I was predisposed to approach real intimacy, when it finally came my way, with the same inquisitive spirit that I demonstrated in less fulfilling relationships. I showed myself that I could learn what intimacy wasn't, and having accomplished that, I could move on to an understanding of what it was. In other words, I was open to growth."

Before proceeding further, let's do a quick recap of the characteristics that define what intimacy is not. It's not:

1. Desperate, craving, wild excitement

2. Imbalanced living

3. A challenge game in which a woman participates in order to "win" a man

4. A high intensity, emotionally overcharged connection to a man

5. A state that you "fall" into. It *is* a state that you can "learn your way" into.

Recognize the Influence of an Unhappy Family Life on Your Own Romantic Destiny

There is a consensus among experts: IF A WOMAN HAS HAD A HAPPY FAMILY LIFE IN CHILDHOOD, SHE IS MUCH MORE LIKELY TO MAKE A HAPPY RO-MANTIC MATCH IN ADULTHOOD. COMING FROM AN UNHAPPY FAMILY PUTS HER AT ROMANTIC RISK. Having discussed this point at length in Chapter II, I don't want to belabor it here except in instances where the voices of the "life experience" experts add new perspectives to the issue or change the slant on it. In reopening this topic, I hope the reader will keep the following facts in mind:

There are gradations and levels of unhappiness in families. No family is as perfect as the sit-coms would have us believe. Real life Huxtables and Bradys don't exist. Some moments of unhappiness are built into the life of every family. Problems develop when unhappiness is a pervasive rather than a fleeting experience for a family member(s).

Sometimes pervasive family unhappiness is subtle—a parent with a mild but chronic depression would be an example. At other times, it's obvious, as in the case where there is an alcoholic parent. In order to cope with either subtle or obvious family unhappiness, children learn to deny or avoid it.

While this may contribute to their emotional survival in childhood, it complicates matters in adulthood because the unacknowledged pain, which has for so long been denied or avoided, finds a way to undermine healthy adult functioning. Romantic relationships are the most likely targets for it. Thus, if a woman finds herself repeatedly entangled in unfulfilling relationships with men, it should be an alert to her that the source of her trouble lies in repressed feelings held over from her family life.

Psychotherapy, then, can be seen and utilized as a way of excavating the repressions, examining them, and then rearranging them so that they no longer need to do their dirty work. Ideally, in the person of the kindly, caring therapist, the client gains a kind of parental surrogate who can, in some measure, compensate for whatever emotional sustenance the parents were unable to provide. Sooner or later, most women who become involved with womanizers find their way to a therapist's door. Again, using the ideal as the standard, it is better if it is sooner rather than later.

Via this detour, I take you now to the main road where some veterans of unhappy families await you:

Julie: "I came from an unhappy family, and from what I've observed, I would say that all women who come from unhappy families have to go to therapy to prevent their relationships with men from being endangered."

Claire: "Women from happy families are not into womanizers. I've noticed this time and time again. They just don't seem to get as hooked on the *chemistry* thing."

June: "I had both alcoholism and divorce in my family. When I was dating womanizers I was unaware of the connection between my family background and my choice of men. I went to therapy. There I learned that the aftereffect of the alcoholism was my tendency to want things to look good on the surface, so if I was with a handsome, successful man, and I was attractive and successful myself, everything was supposed to be OK. It didn't matter whether things felt good. They just had to look good. The aftereffect of the divorce was to make me terrified of abandonment, so I'd do anything to stay in the relationship. Daughters of divorce, especially when it's the father who leaves, often spend the rest of their lives attempting to replay the abandonment drama. They repeat the anguish of it over and over again, and womanizers are the perfect partners, because the threat of abandonment is always there. The fantasy the woman has is that *this time she'll triumph.* She'll get this one to stay."

Emily: "From all appearances, my parents were happily married and devoted to one another, but my mother did have this habit of not talking about problems. She thought it was best to leave things unsaid to avoid creating a disturbance in the orderliness of our family life. My sister and I both married womanizers. Now I think I overlooked my husband's womanizing for so long because some of my mother's personality had rubbed off on me. It's not a good idea for women to sweep problems under the rug for the sake of appearances."

A Womanizer Who Changed
and How It Happened

There were very few stories with happy endings, but Jessica's was an exception: "Womanizing doesn't have to be the most unworkable marital problem. There are worse problems in many marriages," she said. For the benefit of readers, she outlined the step-by-step process that she and her husband went through to rehabilitate their marriage:

Confrontation: "I confronted him and said, 'You've got to stop womanizing.' Women have to confront their husbands about it, but in doing so they should be psychologically prepared to leave the marriage if the husband won't stop his behavior. He has to know that you mean what you say."

Separate your hurt from his problem: "You have to recognize that his problem has nothing to do with you. It is most likely to be related to his early family life."

Healing: "First, you have to get over the hurt, anger, and pain in order to have enough emotional distance to make it clear to him that his behavior is unacceptable. This step is so crucial that you might have to take a break from each other in order to work on your own feelings and to assess whether or not you want to stay in the marriage."

Think about what you'd be losing if you left: "Women shouldn't be so quick to throw a relationship away. With a new person you might have just as many or more problems. When you're in pain you're apt to make impulsive decisions that you might later regret."

See if he's willing to go to counseling: "Counseling will help, because in most instances it will reinforce the fact that womanizing is an unacceptable behavior. Hearing that from a professional person, someone besides his wife, will have an impact on him. It will show him that everybody is attracted to the 'forbidden' in life, and it will force him to ask himself whether the 'fun of the forbidden' is worth wrecking all the other parts of his life."

Ask if the marriage is worth saving: "Is he a decent person, a good father, a good provider, and willing to change his behavior? If you can be satisfied that he meets these criteria, then it's worth the effort to save the marriage."

Jessica was fortunate. She and her husband were able to work together to resurrect their marriage, but it wouldn't have been possible had he been unwilling to stop womanizing. Her most significant contribution to the happy ending was her ability to place herself and her hurt feelings *outside* the province of his problem. By refusing to share blame or responsibility for her husband's behavior, Jessica enabled her husband to diagnose his problem accurately and treat it effectively.

NOTES

CHAPTER I

1. Doris Kearns Goodwin, *The Fitzgeralds and the Kennedys* (New York: St. Martin's Press, 1987), p. 362.

2. Ibid, p. 363.

3. Ibid., pp. 493–494.

CHAPTER II

1. William S. Appleton, M.D., *Fathers and Daughters* (New York: Berkley Books, 1987), p. xiv.

2. Ibid., pp. 13, 14.

3. Ibid., p. 147.

4. Ibid., p. 14.

5. Maggie Scarf, *Intimate Partners* (New York: Ballantine Books, 1987), pp. 151–152.

6. Ibid., p. 153.

CHAPTER III

1. Susan Trausch, *The Boston Globe Sunday Magazine*, November 29, 1987, pp. 76–77.

2. Lawrence Stone in *Passionate Attachments*, ed. Willard Gaylin, M.D., and Ethel Person, M.D. (New York: The Free Press/Macmillan, Inc., 1988), p. 20.

3. William May in *Passionate Attachments*, p. 33.

4. Ibid., p. 36.

5. Willard Gaylin, M.D., *Rediscovering Love* (New York: Penguin Books, 1986), p. 212.

6. Ibid., pp. 212–213.

CHAPTER IV

1. Robin Norwood, *Women Who Love Too Much* (New York: Pocket Books, 1985), p. 6.

CHAPTER V

1. Connell Cowan and Melvyn Kinder, *Smart Women, Foolish Choices*, (New York: Clarkson Potter, Inc., 1985), p. 72.

2. Arianna Stassinopoulos Huffington, "Creator and Destroyer," *The Atlantic*, June 1988, p. 53.

CHAPTER VI

1. Peter Trachtenberg, *The Casanova Complex* (New York: Poseidon Press, Simon & Schuster, 1988), p. 17.

INDEX